Strength

for the

Journey

DR. KASI HOWARD

STRENGTH FOR THE JOURNEY

Copyright © 2019 by Dr. Kasi Howard

Interior Format

To Isabella,
and anyone who is taking the journey of life.
Welcome home to yourself!

To CTC,
thank you for starting the greatest journey of my life.
You are forever my it.

Special thanks to Korby for being an amazing example
of genuine- and for being excited for me, even when I
am crying because you see more than I see.

Thank you to Rosanne for being my fellow sojourner
on this path of life.

Thank you to Justin and
Liz for the feedback and edits. You guys are amazing.

FOREWORD

—◆—

I AM NOT TOO FOND OF forewords because they aren't numbered, so they usually do not feel as if they are officially part of the book. That means that, no matter how long it is, you don't get credit for reading those pages. I find this to be a literary rip-off. When it was suggested to me that I add a foreword to this book, I balked at the idea as it felt unfair to take your time as a reader and not give you credit for pages read. That did not feel like a great way to begin our relationship, and I did not want to do that to you.

Sometimes we have to do things out of necessity to make other things make sense, so here we are. I need to tell you a little about me to help you understand what you are getting into. Therefore, in exchange, I am offering you double credit for reading it. That's right, at the end of this little section, if anyone happens to ask you how far you are in the book, you can say, "I am seven pages in." Now if that feels fair to you- and you are the type of person that cares about that sort of thing- we are going to get along just fine. Welcome to the journey!

I always said I could never write a book. I love speaking and teaching, but I have never imagined

I would have the patience to write anything substantial. Then, one day, a woman of God told me
that I was going to write a book. I laughed and told
God that He had better hook a sister up with some
inspiration if that was going to happen. Then, He
did. I have a habit of arguing with the Almighty
from time to time, so I began to question if I possibly had anything to say about so many different
areas of life, but He seemed to think that I might,
so here we are.

I have been a Clinical Psychologist for over a
decade, so you will inevitably find some free therapy in here. I am also a lover of Jesus, so you will
find a little of Him sprinkled in, too. I had a few
friends read this for me before publishing to get
feedback. One told me that there was a lot of
"Kasi" in here. This is true. You will find a whole
lot of me in here. I have dealt with an eating disorder, depression, suicidality, divorce, emotional
abuse, and I am always freezing. It has been quite
the journey to overcome these things, and I am
incredibly grateful that most of those are a thing
of the past. Except I am still always cold just as a
reminder that I am still a work in progress. From
all of my experiences, I have learned a great deal
about people, life, and most of all, myself.

 Along with the therapy, the Jesus, and all of the
"me," my prayer is that you find a whole lot of
"you" in here, too. If you do, then call me. Primar-
ily if your life these days depends on dry shampoo
because who has time to wash their hair every
week...oops, I meant..day? We should do lunch

because I am sure we could be friends. Just know that I stink at making plans in advance and have never mastered the art of the calendar, so let's make it a spontaneous thing. Also, I do not like Italian food. Now turn to the page so we can start this journey!

Love,

Kasi

CHAPTER 1: ONE DAY

I LIKE TO SAY THAT I am an analogous learner. Stories make things "sticky" in the memory and easier to understand. As my gift to you, I am going to start with one of my best stories. My great uncle had a fake nose that was purely for aesthetic purposes. Apparently, he had cancer and had to have his real nose removed, leaving behind a gaping hole. In place of it lay a prosthetic that he superglued on, one that often melted in the West Texas heat. At any family gathering, my dad and others would be seen walking around searching for JW's nose, which had unknowingly fallen off somewhere. On one memorable occasion, he leaned over my shoulder as I was grabbing a snack, and it fell off right in the center of my donut. He just walked off, not knowing that he left his nose in the circle of my chocolate delight. Sometimes you can be missing something important and not realize it until you feel the draft of a gaping hole in your face, or worse…in your heart.

As a psychologist, I often ask people if they feel depressed. Usually, I get a blank stare in response because "who knows what depression feels like." I explain that it is "a struggle to do things as if your every move is just coated in molasses, and everything is harder than it should be." Then comes the nod of agreement. Unfortunately, for many of you, life has been this way for so long that you no longer identify it as a struggle. It starts to feel like this must be a normal life. Maybe you have even had the thought, "this must be what life is really always like…I was just fortunate that I had not felt it before." Friend, if you have had that thought, let me tell you that this is NOT how you are meant to live your days.

According to a survey of 2,000 Americans, the average person has 15 perfectly happy days per year. The study went on to define the ideal temperature (74°), time of day to wake up (8:15 am) and way to spend the day (outside), with loved ones, and capped off with some tv time on the couch. Sounds pretty solid to me. The good news is that somewhere in those 350 less-than-perfect days, there can be found enough joy to keep one from falling off a ledge. The trick is in finding it.

A bout of deep depression hit me in college following a break up with quite possibly the most boring guy on earth. For example, he didn't want to take the top off of his Jeep because it would ruin the paint on the screws. Mr. Hilarious and I mutually decided to break up nine months later after a long drive in his perfectly topped Jeep. While this ending shouldn't have been a shock, the effect that it had on me was. Somehow, this left me devastated as I had poured all of my energy into him instead of making friends after I had moved to a new town. It was a rookie mistake, but trust me when I say, he was not the cause of my pain. Depression doesn't need a real reason to invade. It just does.

Some days you may feel like you should have a "congratulations" banner hanging in your room when you go to bed for making it through the day. Merely surviving the day was difficult enough to merit more than a participant ribbon. Going to sleep becomes the human equivalent of hitting control-alt-delete. The problem is it only takes about 2.5 seconds from the time your eyes first open in the morning until the reality of the current state of your life comes back and sinks in. And I mean sinks. Deep. Making you want to sink further back into the covers as you are smacked with the reality of a struggle against a force you cannot see or touch but that still hits you like a tidal wave to the soul. The reality of emotions you cannot control or even explain blocks your steps like invisible walls. It's at that moment when THAT reality sinks in that you have a choice: you can choose to roll over and sink deeper into every hurt and ache that you feel, or you can choose to push past those feelings and do the next right thing, which is usually coffee.

I think most of us are more than familiar with the hard days. Those are the days that you wake up and feel you cannot go one more day. For me, when I was struggling, the alarm was just a sad reminder that I had to endure another day. I had an alarm clock which I placed on the other side of the room and turned on full blast with hopes that it would make me get up to go turn it off. Nope. I just let it play as I lay in bed, pondering my existence and how long it would persist. Meanwhile, my neighbor Walter, a 45-year-old exchange student with an appreciation for classical music, wondered why he was stuck living in a duplex with absurdly thin walls next to a girl who never took her mail out of the box and turned the music up at 6 am. Clearly, my misery wanted company. To add to our shared misery, our duplex was overrun with cockroaches the size of your face that I was sure could stage a coup and take over the place at any time. Poor Walter. Poor me. Many days, the alarm would sound "The Middle" by Jimmy Eat World. Somehow, in that song, I found just enough encouragement to get up and brush my teeth. I lived minute by minute, looking for something to carry me from one moment to the next.

As I got older, my dark times got even darker. I would find myself crying on the floor with a handful of pills and a heart full of despair. Still, the same principle carried me. Survive this moment. Find one thing that gives you the strength to get up. Find one thing that makes you want to live for the next thing to come. I remember times where I would listen to a particular song on repeat, literally surviving 3 minutes and 56 seconds at a time until that tidal wave of depression would recede enough for me to catch my breath and reset. Sometimes that's what it takes – one song. One episode of Friends. One chapter. One moment at a time. Keep doing that, and slowly, it builds. Minutes turn to hours. Hours turn to days. And days turn to years. You have to choose to do it. Choose you. Choose hope. Choose life.

Sadly, no one can make this choice for you. I am sure you have people in your life who wish they could. They watch you, wondering what they can do to convince you life isn't so bad, or how they can love you enough to make you love yourself. It's not about them or what they can or can't do. It has never been. This is a common misnomer. Depression is not about a balance sheet of pluses and minuses, tabulating the things that have gone wrong in your life and the things that are going well. In fact, for those who have long struggled, there is usually an amount of shame that comes with the struggle as they are continuously told to focus on the good instead and "count their blessings." While that is a great practice to adopt, it does not provide an answer to all questions of suffering. There isn't a formula to determine if you are allowed to be upset and to what degree. No matter how high you count, it still doesn't add up. It doesn't explain the pain. Call it "a chemical imbalance." Call it "seasonal" because the sun didn't come out enough today. Call it "situational" because you missed a BOGO sale at The Rack. I don't know why you are hurting. And, I also don't know why your cousin's mother's friend's neighbor went through the same situation and seems unscathed. Depression and struggle don't play by rules of logic, and they don't play fair.

Modern psychology would tell us to change our thought patterns and learn to fight that "stinkin' thinking." While this can be effective, what if there's more to gaining a life of joy and victory than just the way we think? What if it involves your core beliefs? The very meaning to which you assign not only to the things that happen to you but to your role in the world around you?

Saying this makes many people cringe as they may have grown up with uncompassionate others telling them if they just trusted God, they would be fine. Or if they were just more grateful for what they do have, they wouldn't be so focused on what they don't. What I mean, what if there is more to your situation, emotions, and experience than what you see in front of you? You have a purpose, and it is probably far more significant than you can fathom right now. There is a reason you are here, right now, in this place. You touch a unique circle of people that no one else in the world touches in the way that you do. You are a gift. And you have a gift.

I believe your Creator intended you to use that gift for His glory- and for your life of abundant joy and meaning. I also honestly believe we have an enemy who wants to destroy that gift (John 10:10) and keep it from ever coming to fruition. That enemy is VERY afraid you will realize who you are, what you have to offer the world around you, and your ability to do amazing things in this life. So he pulls out every possible stop to keep you from accomplishing your mission. He uses everything from winter months and wayward spouses, to angry mothers and a never-ending pile of bills and even other spiritual leaders. This produces voices so loud in your head, voices that drown out the truth of who you are and what you are meant to

The thief comes only to steal + kill + destroy; I have come that they may have life,

do. From a tactical perspective, it's brilliant. It has worked since the beginning of time.

No amount of talent, fame, or notoriety can inoculate you from those voices. Even winning enough gold medals to make new earrings for the Real Housewives of the OC, New York, and Atlanta combined doesn't guarantee confidence. I love me some Michael Phelps. The most decorated Olympian of all time, he has had his share of battles. Going into the 2012 Olympics, where he won 4 gold and 2 silver medals, he describes himself as having "no self-confidence and no self-love." After winning, he goes on to say, "I was in the lowest place I've ever been. Honestly, I sort of, at one point, I just, I felt like I didn't want to see another day. I felt like it should be over." Gold medals, Wheaties boxes, and the high honor of being my celebrity crush did not make him feel like he had a purpose of continuing in this life. He bought into the lie of worthlessness, like so many of us are today. We compare ourselves to our peers, colleagues, and even our own imagined idea of where we thought we would be right now. Add in modern-day social media, where a comparison is just a click away, and we are all suddenly carrying a potential mental Hiroshima in our pockets wherever we went.

———◆———

I have the privilege of hearing many stories in my practice as a clinical psychologist. As I listened to a woman cry and talked about her years of depression and suffering, how she had been beaten up over the years by these constant attacks was almost tangible. After suffering so long, she bought into the lie that this is her life and her battle to wage without end. Whether it be emotional or political, truth is the first casualty of war.

Many battles have been won and lost by deception. During the Civil War, "Stonewall" Jackson led a force of 16,000 men that were suddenly caught in the middle of 52,000 converging Union soldiers. If the Union had been aware of their real advantage, they would have crushed Jackson's forces. However, Jackson sent infiltrators to spread rumors that his troops were in the six digits. As the Union closed in on both sides of him, Jackson marched his army from one side of the valley to another until Lincoln ordered a withdraw of Union troops, believing they were grossly outnumbered. Maybe you feel outnumbered because you have over-estimated the size of the forces against you. Though they seem countless, they do have a limit. Your shameful thoughts, anxious fears, and even the very tears that you cry, pale in comparison to the strength, courage, and tenacity that you possess. The next question is: Are you ready for a recount?

———•———

You must decide for yourself that you are going to pursue your purpose relentlessly and refuse to buy into the lies that you will always suffer or that your highs will only be "not as lows." When ghosts from your past remind you of previous "failures," you must silence them with the power of your purpose. When guilt and shame shout that you are not good enough, you must shout back that you are on a mission and you don't have time to listen to them anymore. It will not be easy at first, but once you are committed, you will figure out how to do it. We will learn some strategies together as you read. Start here: What resources do you have inside you to make the very long step from the top of your bed to the floor...twice – once with each foot? Good luck.

Although I cannot tell you what superpowers you have that will help you leap to your feet and greet the day as if you were an annoyingly perfectly put together Instagram icon, I can give you a few suggestions:

When you feel like you cannot go one more day, remember that you did, in fact, get through yesterday. Perhaps it was difficult, but you did it. Over the years, I have run many marathons and half marathons (Side note: there is nothing "half" about 13.1 miles.) Regardless of the finish time, at the end the race you get a finisher medal. It doesn't matter if you were first across the line or if you limped across as everyone was packing up for the day, you still get a medal. As someone hands you a cold towel and a bottle of water, you feel like a champion for that one moment just because you made it. We all have those days where we feel like we should get a medal just for finishing, despite it not being pretty. There's an old joke that says,

"What do you call a doctor who made all D's in med school?... 'Doctor!'" Quit judging yourself because you didn't leap through the day with ease and grace. You did it, and it's done. Congratulations.

Though it is not a cure-all, changing your perspective to focus on the good can make a huge difference. Take some time to name the things for which you are grateful — all of them. The small ones are the ones that often get overlooked but are the little things that make a day worth living. If you think about it, you have one wedding day (we hope), maybe a few days that your kids are born (unless you are my sister, who has seven kids,... in that case you have an entire weeks' worth), and maybe a few promotions or killer hair days in between. Otherwise, life is mostly a lot like Groundhog Day. Every day, I wake up, feed my dogs, make my breakfast, brush my teeth, wash my face, put my contacts in and so on. Every. Frickin'. Day. Literally. That never changes. If I am waiting for Ed Sheeran waking me up with a sweet good morning song to be my reason to get out of bed, I am going to be sadly disappointed, over and over again. If I wake up and am thankful that my heater is working and that my dogs haven't puked in the night, then life starts to look a little brighter. It's not about settling or lowering your standards. It's about perspective. Try looking a little closer at the details of each day's art instead of whizzing through the gallery like a speed walker in the mall. Slow down and window shop a little. You might see something you like.

Laundry sucks. Why? Because we see it as a task to be done. Somewhere along the way, we gave a whole other name to clothes that need to be cleaned or were just cleaned. Now it's a chore, and most people don't like doing it. At what point does that new pair of jeans that you love become laundry that you hate? Somewhere your frame of mind has shifted. It needs to shift back. Be grateful for little feet that make dirty socks, jeans that make your butt look better, and a bed that is covered in sheets that make sleeping cozier, especially if they are t-shirt sheets. Those sheets rock and deserve extra gratitude.

When you are struggling, make your own list. When I do this, I literally write them down on a sheet of paper. Usually, I start by looking up for a moment to solidify that I am taking a different view. Also, I painted my ceiling a few months ago, so I get excited to see how super bright white it is. That often begins my list. Item 1: A bright white ceiling. When you look up from where you are, the view changes. And sometimes, what we need more than anything is to see something different. A glimpse of hope that things won't always be like this pause for a minute and make a list of things that made you smile today. That change in perspective alone can change your view enough to buy you another day.

There's a Mr. Rogers meme that gets circulated after something awful happens that says, "Look for the helpers. There is always someone trying to help when something bad happens." I have found this to be true. In 2017, the largest mass shooting in U.S. history happened in Las Vegas in the middle of a country music festival. That was horrifically tragic as many lives were lost in an instant. But what happened afterward was almost just as beautiful as the event was horrific. People around the country began offering support to those affected and their families. Facebook groups were created in which people were offering strangers a place to stay, clothes to wear, and a ride home. People with private planes offered them up to help victims, and their families reunite. It was a selfless outpouring of love that the media almost completely ignored as it focused on the gravity of the loss. The reality is that, in any tragedy, there is a multitude of voices whispering love that drowned out a few loud voices of hatred. We have to tune our ears to hear them.

I hear horror stories all day long about the trauma that people have endured at the hands of others. I am not minimizing those stories. I am also not here to tell you that you endured what you did for some greater good. That is seriously one of my biggest gripes about well-meaning Christians who want to wrap your agony in a bow and say it was God's plan. I completely disagree with that. There is certainly an evil that exists in the world, and you have probably felt the brunt of it, my friend. We have all felt unseen or unheard by someone at some time. I am here to tell you that if you expand the perspective a little further out, there is usually someone trying to help. Love can be found in any story. Once you find it, it is like finding Waldo – you cannot unsee it. You start to notice the random act of kindness or grace written on every page. It doesn't undo the sadness, but it makes it more bearable to know that someone cared. Someone tried to help in some way. There was a balance of good to the bad that you could not see at that moment. It's all about perspective and being able to broaden your view of any situation.

Perception is a funny thing. While eating lunch, my friend's precious 5 year old daughter ran to give me a gift that she had picked up on the playground. She handed me what she saw as a beautiful patterned treasure- but what was clearly an insect wing. I stared at it, wanting to receive her gift of love but very much not wanting to touch a piece of a dead bug as I was about to gnaw into my cheeseburger. I gently took it with the tiniest grip of my fingers possible and and accepted it for what she intended it to be and not what it appeared to be to me. Sometimes the intention has to outweigh the disguise.

Sometimes when you feel you cannot go one more day, try finishing the sentence to be more precise and gain some clarity. "I cannot go one more day_____." Maybe you cannot go one more day in your job, with your partner or without a partner, or with no money. There is always an end to the sentence, but we tend to leave it off that makes us feel as if a change is out of our reach. It's not. The reality is you are not a tree. You can move. You can break up. You can make up. You can put on make-up. You can get a new job or go back to school. We spend a lot of time using our misery as an excuse instead of looking for a way out of it. Let me tell you; there is almost always a way out of it unless you are on the east coast and in dire need of a Diet Dr. Pepper. That is usually just a desperate and hopeless situation.

To make a change, you have to finish the sentence and identify what is making you miserable. Once you do that, you need a game plan to make it better. We will explore some of those options later, but for now, let's talk basics.

Let's say you wake up and feel that you cannot go one more day in this relationship. What do you do? How can you fix a situation like that? You cannot change those around you. However, you can change your interactions with them. Just like people in a play follow a script, we follow a script with those around us. For example, at this point, you don't need to start the argument with your mate to know how it's going to end. We all have our "greatest hits," those things that we fight about over and over. You could act out both parts and be pretty close to verbatim on the script of reality. But what would happen if you changed YOUR line? If Luke doesn't say, "You killed my father," Darth Vader can't say "I am your father." When one person changes their lines, the other person must do the same.

No matter what the situation, there are things you can do to change it — even just a little. A tiny change one day can be just enough to get your feet on the ground the next. Just enough to give you the energy to get back in there.

The two most hopeful words in the English language are "one day." That's all it takes. Tomorrow could be your "one day." It could be the one day that everything changes. One day, you will get the promotion, meet Mr. or Mrs. Right, or reach the breaking point of an old addiction. And you never know when that day will come. So get up, put those feet on the ground and remember that "one more day" could turn into your "one day" today.

"One moment can change a day. One day can change a life. And one life can change the world."
~ Buddha

CHAPTER 2: AIN'T NO SUCH THING AS A MISTAKE

E VER WONDER WHY PENS HAVE a hole at the end of the cap? It seems like a useless feature at best, and counter-productive at worst, as it would allow more air into the tip, potentially drying it out faster. But swallowing pen lids was a big enough problem that someone added the hole so the unfortunate party can still breathe while awaiting medical attention. That little hole has a significant purpose, just like every person on this earth has a purpose. Even all those accidental pen cap swallowers.

The purpose is such a vague- yet grandiose- word; it can often seem too big to attain and too overwhelming to even try. Asking yourself, "What is my purpose?" sounds not only difficult to answer but possibly pretentious to even ask. Most of the time we don't even know what purpose looks like, but we are sure when we lack it, and indeed, we will know it when we find it. To keep us all on the same page, I looked up the definition of purpose, which reads "the reason for which something is done or created or for which something exists." Pretty lofty, eh? Wrap your mind around that. We are all searching for the REASON we exist on this earth.

I do not believe this is a BAD question to ask. In fact, in many respects, you could say it is your JOB as a human to find your purpose and do it. The problem is that we tend to add layers of judgment on ourselves for not finding it, or not finding it fast enough or not being instantly good at it that we end up missing it altogether. In the same way, many of us chastise ourselves for not having the job we thought we would have by the time we turned this many years and condemn ourselves for not fulfilling some noble ideal sense of meaning that we have created out of thin air.

I used to work with people with eating disorders, spending countless hours helping people make peace with food and their bodies. After years of working with patients to find their identity that the disorder stole, it finally hit me: eating disorders are just a passive way to die. Depression, anxiety, self-harm, eating disorders, and substance use—all of it comes from a place of not wanting to live in this moment as it is. This is not suicidality. There is a difference in wanting to die and not wanting to be alive. This passive attitude about your existence is more like driving without a seatbelt. Whatever happens, happens. I believe this apathy for life develops when we start asking "why am I here?" and we can't find an answer.

I want to take you on a journey with me through how I found my purpose and walk with you as you find yours. I may not have all the answers, but I can tell you that I know I have a purpose. So do you. Settle in, buckle up -because you are worth it- and get ready to find meaning in life again.

Every story is different, so I am going to tell you mine in general terms with hopes that you can relate in some way. I used to wake up most days feeling overwhelmed by what was in front of me. There was so much good I wanted to do. I knew what I was capable of and what I could be doing. Somehow I fell short, day after day. The things I was doing didn't seem to mean anything. They were not enough. I was in a helping profession. I adopted a child. I rescued two dogs, one of which still thanks me by peeing on my floor regularly. I tithed, giving a regular percentage of my income to the church, no matter my financial situation. I recycled. I flossed my teeth every day. I didn't take excessive napkins at fast food places. And I usually picked up trash on the sidewalk. None of that made me believe that living my life was worth the pain that I felt. It all felt pointless. For years, I could not see a need for me to be here, and if I am perfectly honest, I couldn't remember if I ever had a purpose.

Yet, during this time, I felt like I was a reasonably good person. I was doing things "right," whatever that meant. Then one day, I started to feel terribly uncomfortable in my life of rule-following. I didn't want to get it all "right" anymore. I was tired of recycling and only using the right size paper towel to avoid being wasteful. Suddenly, I felt like the imaginary walls I had built in my life to give me structure were closing in on me. It became too much, and I sort of flipped out, and I did things I am not proud of. I quit flossing. And I hurt people that I love.

I began to feel shame. I'm not talking about guilt like you feel when you buy a ridiculously expensive pair of jeans because those girls at The Buckle convinced you that they make your butt look amazing. Guilt and shame are very different. Guilt says I DID something wrong, while shame says I AM something wrong, a bad person or defective in some way. Guilt can be healthy, as it often leads to making amends and correcting behaviors. Shame is never healthy. It leads to condemnation, depression, self-hatred, and despair.

Shame can be felt emotionally, mentally, and physically. It becomes a mask that we wear. Physically, I feel shame on my face, like an actual layer of wrong being, separating me from the world. Perhaps you, too, feel it is slathered on your face for all the world to see. Maybe you feel it in the pit of your stomach eating away at you. Stop for a minute and ask yourself where you feel your shame. _____*face + body*_____. It's important to identify where we carry our shame physically, as well as mentally, so we can recognize it when it crops up. Being able to label this emotion is step one in overcoming its soul-consuming effects.

We then need to recognize the function that it serves. Your shame is a big, comfy security blanket.

It gives you a sense of safety because it preserves the balance of good and bad in the world. If you were an awful person or did something horrible, it would explain and justify the appalling things that happened to you. It protected you from believing that the world was harsh. If good things can happen to good people, then the world becomes a very unsafe place. But if bad things only happen to bad people, then the world is predictable and just, making it feel safer. If the people around you were not taking responsibility for their hurtful actions, intentional or not, then justice says that someone had to. Like in the Hunger Games, someone had to volunteer as tribute to make things "right." Thus enters shame. It takes you from being a victim to being judge, jury, and executioner. Shame provides a sense of control in a situation that seemed uncontrollable by placing the onus of responsibility on yourself. If you are "certain it was your fault," then you can be sure justice is served, and corrective actions are taken. Thus shame serves as an insurance policy that says that it won't happen again, no matter what "it" is.

The roots of shame lie in assuming debt that was never entirely yours. Think of it like this: Event A happens to me. If I blame myself, I get to continue to believe that the world is a just place – something bad happened to someone bad. That feels fair, and I can live with that more easily than if I have to think bad things happen to good people. I can also ensure that someone pays the price, i.e., me. With every self-loathing thought that goes through my head, justice is carried out. All of this preserves my worldview and keeps me from having to face the hard truths that sometimes good people suffer, and sometimes others get away with causing that suffering. Shame serves a role, though the costs of this safety blanket far outweigh the benefits.

Research shows that shame is the number one contributor to stress, even more than working excessively. It is stifling. Shame produces an emotional fight, flight, or freeze response. It leads an individual to manage negative emotions by taking power over another or being aggressive; to withdraw and avoid the situations that could produce it thus becoming isolated, or to work excessively hard to please others and to seek to belong.

Sometimes "flight" can look a lot like "fight." I went through a time where my heart was very guarded. I had been hurt many times as I realized too late that someone was not the person they first claimed to be. Quite frankly, I was tired of experiencing heartache. It was not an intentional choice to not trust others, but rather a product of experience. I had fallen for someone who appeared to be kind and loving for a few months and then turned into Mr. Hyde overnight, ultimately becoming emotionally and mentally abusive. Therefore, I was not "fooled" by someone being nice to me. I knew that there could be icy layers underneath deep enough to sink the Titanic. God bless the guy who wanted to date me during this time. I was always on guard, watching for signs of his "true colors." Instead, I missed that I was wearing red glasses the entire time, automatically tinting his words to be a different color. While there is some wisdom in allowing people time to prove themselves worthy of your affection, we must make sure that we are working to see people clearly and not through our lenses of distrust, anger and hurt.

Just like Adam and Eve suddenly became aware of their nakedness and hid from God, when we become aware of our shortcomings, we begin to hide from those that we love. We don't want them to see our naked imperfections. This withdrawal from others now compounds our shame as we feed our self-hatred by cutting ourselves off from people and activities that could feed our self-esteem and build us up. When I avoid other people, I may prevent them from hurting me, but I also lose the opportunity to let them love me. It also expands the impact of our shame to those around us, costing them what could have been a beautiful relationship with us, as well. This further fuels negativity and hurt in our world. And the beat goes on. All of these responses shift the focus away from personal growth and progress to a state of emotional triage, working tirelessly to stop the constant barrage of self-deprecating thoughts.

Believing that I AM defective caused all motivation to better my life to come to a screeching halt. I tried to embrace my Plan B, this new life that was a product of poor choices. I drank a little more than I should have. I sought affection in places I was never going to find it. I gave up lifelong dreams, and I allowed myself to forego long-held values because I was no longer good enough to live up to them anyway. I moved from guilt to shame, then to despair, where I set up camp.

In the Screwtape Letters by C. S. Lewis, Uncle Screwtape is a demon, coaching his nephew on how to discourage a Christian on Earth. He says if you can exacerbate shame enough, you will produce despair. Despair will show a man that he was only able to so willingly accept God's grace and forgiveness for his other mistakes only because he did not truly understand their sinfulness. Once he truly understands the full depth of what he has done, he cannot accept mercy for it. Simply put, it is easy to believe in grace until you think you need it. The most significant way to destroy a person's faith – and a sense of purpose – is to convince him that he has done something too big to be forgiven.

If left unchecked, shame will quickly produce despair that can shackle you. I was a "good enough" person until I did something I believed was truly bad. Then suddenly, I was beyond redemption. I felt I had ruined any hope I had of making a difference in the world. In my mind, I had permanently altered my path in such a way that it could never lead anywhere worthwhile. I lost my purpose.

The thing that kept me trying at all was my hope that, even if my life was ruined, perhaps I could feed enough goodness into my son that he could do something good for the world. I was trying to pass on the last Lorax seed to make up for all the forests I had chopped down for my own "thneeds." My chance was gone; he was not. This caused many issues. For example, it meant that my son being upset with me was devastating, as it was the last shred of purpose I had. As any parent knows, you are not doing your job if your child is not at least occasionally upset with you, so in fulfilling my role as a parent, I was adding to my own misery. My hope for life would come and go with the passing whims of a seven-year-old.

I had a solidly held belief that I had no purpose, which I did not think could ever change; therefore, I didn't even try to change it. That would have been like trying to convince me that Hitler was just misunderstood or that french fries count as a vegetable. No sense spending hours trying to change facts. Though I hated how I viewed myself, I did not believe it was something I could change. Feeling resolved to accept my new fate as a useless screw-up, I just tried to make the best of it.

If you're like me, there is a list of awful things about yourself that you believe right now. Whether it is because of your actions or the hurts others have inflicted upon you; you are embracing your "ruined fate." Maybe like me, you once believed you had a great Plan A. Maybe you never had that luxury. Perhaps you have always thought that you are worthless and you will never do much more than pass time in this life. Let me echo the voice of your Creator and tell you that those are lies from the enemy. Your life, the very breath that you take now, has value. Your job has never been to survive days or pass the time. You are meant for more. You are intended to capture each moment and use it for a higher purpose, both for you and others. So was I, but I didn't know that then.

There I was, busy just passing time, riding around without a seatbelt when I had an encounter with God that changed everything. After a particularly awful night of battling thoughts of uselessness, I met a friend at a Bible study to ask for prayer. The pastor told me that God saw my broken heart and the weight I was carrying, and He no longer wanted me to shut the door on painful memories. He wanted me to face my past and learn to rejoice in it. God then began to reveal to my heart what my head had always prevented me from believing. My life was not on a second-rate, Plan B course, as I had convinced myself. It was still part of His holy Plan A which had never changed. You see, my friend, "mistakes" ARE part of the plan, not a deviation from it. The plan has never been that you would get everything right all along, nor was it that everyone would get everything right with you. That is simply unrealistic.

I hear you saying that YOUR mistakes are too big to be part of the plan – or perhaps the mistakes others made against you are. But God's plan is too big to be altered by your missteps. Errors are not things that are NOT supposed to happen. They are things that we realize later we could have done better. Read that again. Just because you see it as a mistake does NOT mean that it should never have happened. It means that you have now grown enough to see a better way to do it. It means that you have learned that it was not the best path. The sheer fact that you were aware of a mistake means that you are a little wiser than before. THAT is how life is supposed to go. We are continually growing and learning.

———————

My sweet son is a bit of a perfectionist. He gets so angry at himself when things don't go right. And, this may shock you, but I am not a perfect mother. So I often tell him, "Have you ever been ten before? Then how on earth are you supposed to know how to be 10?! And I have never been a mother to a 10-year-old, so I am not going to get that right every time." We must learn to give ourselves grace. You have never done this human thing before, so why do you think you should nail every aspect the first time?

Though we are not born with the ability to see the best possible path in every situation, perhaps your shame is because you DID know the right choice and didn't make it. This was the case for me. Though I'm not condoning or excusing this type of decision making, it, too, is inevitable. Some days we struggle to find the resources to do what we know we should. Most people are doing the best they can with what they have. They might lack the emotional, financial, relational, or physical resources to do anything different in the moment. I frequently remind my clients that they did not choose to have an eating disorder or an addiction because it sounded like fun. Instead, they found their capacity to cope with the pressures or temptations of life insufficient and turned to an alternative that would keep the painful emotions under control. Or at least the illusion of control. Thus it worked. The problem is that the costs of this way of coping far outweigh the benefits and quickly become another issue that must be a.

If you genuinely trace back through the actions that likely led to your "mistake," you will inevitably find that they began in a situation that you did not recognize at the time was "wrong." I frequently do "behavior chains" with my clients. In these exercises, we take the end action that they wish to change, and we ask what happened just before that, and before that, and before that. Most often, the problem behavior was not a result of the event that occurred immediately before it. Events don't cause emotions. Our interpretation of them does. This is why it is also essential to identify vulnerability factors. These are things that prevent us from being on our "A-game" like being hungry, tired, angry, lonely, or bored. In a broader sense, vulnerability factors can also be messages you received as a child that told you that you were worthless; generational shame passed down from a mother who believed she was not good enough; the loss of a key person in your life, etc. These things, along with so much more, keep us from making decisions that reflect our best selves. They make us vulnerable to believing lies about ourselves and our potential. These unaddressed chinks in our armor are most often where the roots of our "mistakes" lie.

The good news is that identifying our vulnerability factors can help us begin to build compassion and understanding for ourselves. No matter where your shame begins, the reality is that we are all generally doing the best we can with what we have. For what we lack, there is grace. Grace is far bigger than your mistakes. Grace is a funny thing. It is not pushy. It does not consume everything in its path like shame. Grace is a gentleman. It requires an invitation. It may feel scary to invite grace in. It is foreign. It is kind and not like the pain you are so accustomed to carrying that condemns. Once inside, however, grace can whitewash every stain and glue together every broken piece left by shame and despair. Grace and shame cannot coexist in the same space. When one enters, the other must leave. Though it may feel scary, it's time to open the door to grace and allow it to clean the messy film that shame has left on your reflection.

I am here to tell you are NOT meant to live this life of shame and regret. It took me years to finally know that in my soul. It took me years to see that whatever I had done could never outweigh what I COULD do. I began by learning that we were never meant to get it all right. Let me help you. You will hurt people you love. You will blow opportunities. You will mismanage finances. You will leave when you should have stayed and stayed when you should have left. You will run into walls, burn popcorn, wreck cars and forget you left a can of soda in the freezer until it explodes all over everything. This is all part of life. There is simply no way around it. Don't be surprised by it. Don't waste any more precious time regretting those things than you spend regretting your unfortunate choice of hairstyle in 4th grade. It is all part of the human experience and learning how to live. After all, what would life be without an embarrassing school photo to remind you that perms are not for everyone?

Once you acknowledge that there is no way you can know how to do life perfectly when you've never done it before, you can begin to embrace the road that you have traveled. It's your road. No one else has ever walked your same path. You have left tracks no one else could leave. As C.S. Lewis said, "Experience is a brutal teacher. But you'll learn, by God, you'll learn." You can hear the pain of the lessons he learned in his words. I can feel the pain in your heart as you read it.

Now, what do you do with all those lessons you're learning? You find your purpose. Don't miss this: Your purpose lies in your ability to take the pain that you have endured and use it as a lesson. A lesson for you. A lesson for your children. For the masses. For ages. It doesn't matter how far it extends. What matters is that, by God, you learn the lesson! Don't stop living your best life because of the brutal experience required to learn it. Don't let your shame turn into despair because you will lose your purpose. In the absence of purpose, we are all driving without a seatbelt, waiting for time to pass and life to let us go. Instead, let us welcome in grace with open arms. In the light of grace, "mistakes" become part of our journey, taking us from one turn in the road to the next.

Listen, friend, it is time you forgive yourself. It is time to stop blaming yourself for the actions of others. It is time you let go of the pain of your past. You were never meant to carry your painful experiences from one part of life to the next. Lay them down. Recognize the lessons that they taught you. Buckle up and allow yourself to dream again.

"If I must start somewhere, right here and now is the best place, imaginable."
~ Richelle E. Goodrich

CHAPTER 3: OPENING YOUR GIFT

M Y SON LIKES TO WATCH these "life hacker"YouTube videos that suggest all sorts of exciting ways to repurpose things rather than discard them. My all-time favorite was a woman who took a pair of men's boxer briefs and turned them into a sports bra.

I am all aboard the money-saving, shabby chic train and all, but I draw the line at using a tired old crotch covering to secure the girls while I run. Sometimes things served their purpose, and they are done. They had a good life, and now they deserve to go to the excellent cotton burial ground in the landfill. The great news is this: You are not a pair of stretched out underwear. You are not done. Your future is still filled with purpose. In fact, my guess is that you are just getting started.

Do you ever have the feeling that you were meant for something more? That you are supposed to make a difference in the world? It is time to lay down your shame and open your eyes to the fact that you have a purpose in this life. The existence of your purpose isn't up for debate. You must realize this truth and grab onto it with every fiber of your being. However, to do this, we need to get a clearer picture of what it is. Which brings us back to the question, what is the purpose? Remember that our definition tells us purpose is "the reason for something's existence." Let's be clear. There are probably a million reasons you were put on this earth. According to Ephesians 2:10, "He prepared good works in advance for us to do." Not just one work, plural works and likes lots of them. While some of us may be blessed with a theme for our lives in which those good works play out, most of us are not. You may not be the one who dedicates your entire life to curing cancer or opening orphanages. Starting an orphanage is noble, though it's just as beautiful to take a child into your home to love as your very own. There are a million ways you can make a difference right where you are that have just as much meaning as the big-ticket acts on which we place so much value.

While everyone's purpose is different, they all share one commonality: people. No one can find their purpose in isolation, nor can they live it out. It will always include others. Here's the excellent news: someone else's purpose also includes you. We are all walking this winding human road together. The more we realize that we are connected and have something to offer our fellow sojourners, the easier the journey becomes for everyone.

To narrow your options, ask yourself, what makes my heartburn with passion? Kids? The elderly? The plethora of stray cats in your neighborhood? Don't judge the answer if it doesn't feel "lofty" enough. I personally hate cats – and I am also allergic, which means I get to blame my avoidance on the hives they cause instead of my own cold heart. It works out. Your heart for them saves me from feeling guilty that I don't care that much about stray cats. Thank you. But I do love teenagers, particularly those who are rebellious and hard to love: the more attitude and the harder the exterior, the better. So while you help the cats, I'll help the angry teens. You're welcome. I have a friend who has made it her mission to be a "strawvangelist," educating people everywhere she goes about the dangers of plastic straws and handing out metal ones. It is a niche market in which she is making a difference, one straw at a time. If everyone followed their natural desires to help, every child, animal, and park would find new life. Instead, if I spend my time trying to fulfill YOUR calling, then those in my circle remain untouched, and I find myself unfulfilled and losing in the game of comparison. The truth is, you look much better in your shoes than I do.

The butterfly effect is a concept that states that small causes can have more substantial effects. It was developed by Edward Lorenz who gave a metaphorical example of the intensity of a tornado being affected by a butterfly flapping its wings three weeks earlier. Thus, a small butterfly can have a rather significant impact on the world. Though this may sound extreme, it plays out in virtually every area of life. Helping a tired mother pick up her fallen groceries could be the encouragement she needed to make it through that day. Making eye contact with the cashier instead of being on your phone can make him feel seen. These tiny acts are what make the human existence beautiful. Once you recognize that we are all intertwined, then even the smallest acts take on more meaning. You never know what great things the person you help will go on to do. Johann Gottlieb Fichte says that "you could not remove a single grain of sand from its place without thereby ... changing something throughout all parts of the immeasurable whole." You could be the one to move the one grain of sand that was blocking a multitude of blessings from pouring out through generations. You must begin to think of the small things as being so much bigger as you follow your heart.

It is miraculous how much passion can fuel greatness to create something extraordinary. For

example, I have an AMAZING church. We don't
have a worship band; we use CDs that sometimes
don't play. We have 1–2 people with a passion for
singing, and if they aren't there, then someone else
steps up to the microphone. We consider ourselves
a training center, which means that people often
preach their very first sermon ever there to give
them a taste of the pulpit. It's in someone's house,
and one time the AC went out. In August. In South
Texas. Since it isn't the seamless worship, the experienced teaching or the lavish facilities, do you
know what makes my church amazing? The people! The hearts! Every person who steps up to that
pulpit or microphone does it with the most amazing heart to serve God that I have ever seen! As a
result, people get delivered and saved and renewed
every week. I have never experienced anything like
it. Because what makes it amazing isn't in anything
specific to MY church (e.g., no huge building,
fancy lighting, or awe-inspiring sanctuary), you
can experience the same thing right where you
are. You need to show up and expect God to move.
Bring your heart. All of it. Bring your passionate
desire for "more," whatever that "more" is what
you need at THIS moment. You don't need a fantastic drummer or an eloquent pastor for that. So
often we waste so much time waiting to be "better," or "ready" that we miss the opportunities that
will get us there. You just need a heart to serve, to
lead, and to receive.

As you figure out what makes your heartbeat, the
next question becomes what to do about it. What
gifts and talents do you have? Unless you are one

of those fantastic right-brained folks with artistic or musical abilities, you may have no idea. When I was in college, I received my all-time favorite backhanded compliment. My roommate thoughtfully shared that she had been feeling down on herself because she did not feel she had any real talents until she got this gem of a revelation: "It hit me that you don't have any talents and people still like you, so it must be okay." Honestly, (and she was brutally honest), she had a point. If we limit our definition of talent to being able to write, sing, or draw, then I don't have any of those. Maybe you don't either. And that's okay. A 2012 study found that only 52% of Americans felt they had a creative ability, and only 25% of those surveyed thought they were living up to their creative potential. That leaves 75% of us suffering from a chronic case of the "not enoughs."

The "not enoughs" can be paralyzing. They tell us that since we aren't doing enough, what we are doing doesn't matter. Those thoughts can kill motivation. If it doesn't matter, why bother? I would like to submit the "one less" mindset instead. Every tear you dry for a grieving friend is one less tear that falls on an empty pillow. Every hug you give is one less minute without human connection for someone. Every time you pick up a piece of litter on the ground, there's one less piece of trash to be seen. Though, for real y' all, I have to wonder who still thinks it is kosher to throw their french fry box out of the car window as if the entire planet is your trash can — moving on....

Though my well-meaning (I think) friend did not know I had any talents, I disagree. I am a good friend. I love people like it's my job. And that talent looks stunning hanging on my walls in the form of pictures of myself with people that I love. I also love to teach. Beth Moore once offered that if every time you learn something new, you feel the need to share it with others, you must be a teacher. I often have to hold back from stopping mid-revelation to post on Facebook or text a close friend because I am so eager to share whatever it is that I am learning. It just took me a while to learn to label this as an actual gift and not just an outlet for my extraversion. Everyone has gifts; they only come in different packages.

Ask yourself where your brain naturally leads. Do you find yourself doing math in your head at random events to calculate the costs? You are a critical thinker. Do you love to connect people? You are a networker. Can you imagine things as better than they are now? You are a visionary. Maybe you are funny. You make people laugh. Trust me; not everyone is a hoot. Can you walk in a room and see how space could have been better arranged or organized? You are an organizer. Maybe you are one of the rare few who can sit with someone in their pain. You are a listener- and quite frankly a saint, in my opinion. All of these ARE talents. Not everyone has these abilities. Take a moment and ask yourself, what are your natural thought patterns. These are your talents. They are useful, and there is a place for them to be used in your present circle.

It is also worth adding that sometimes your purpose is not a what, per se, but a when. I love the story of Esther. She was a servant girl chosen to be King Xerxes' new Queen after Queen Vashti got the boot. One of the King's right-hand men, Hamon, was going to convince him to annihilate the Jews, who were Esther's people. Because of her place with the King, she was able to expose Hamon's plan and convince the King not to annihilate her people. It was indeed "for such a time as this" (Esther 4:14) that she found her purpose. Don't overlook the power of life's seasons. Maybe you are currently called to be a mother and focus on your children. Perhaps you have been placed in a job where you can influence someone of power. The right word at the right time can change a life. Who knows but that "for such a time as this" you have not been placed right where you need to be to change the course of your world?

I think most of us have an idea of what makes us special, but we tend to minimize it as if it doesn't matter. We write off our gift of service as something "anyone would do." Let me tell you, not just anyone COULD do it, and I guarantee you not everyone WOULD do it. For example, I have a friend, Lisa, that only shows up with a casserole to be a blessing. She does not limit herself to do this for funerals and births. She does it when someone is sick. She does it when someone loses a job. She does it because it is Monday and she knows you have no idea how you will make it through this week. That is a GIFT! I will tell you a secret: I can cook one meal. I make a rather impressive pan of enchiladas. Other than that…I got nothing. So if I have brought you enchiladas in recent history, then I have nothing else to offer. I am thankful for the Lisas of the world who make up for my lack of culinary breadth. I have another friend who texted me almost every morning for a year saying that she was praying for me. Y'all, waking up to that was my lifeline! I sincerely hope that she did not for a minute doubt or minimize the effects of her prayers or texts. They are more of a gift than a thousand bouquets of flowers. Think of the things that others have complimented you on, even if you have not fully received those compliments with the acceptance that they merit. Just because you cannot see the value of the good they do in the moment, does not mean it does not exist. Opportunities to serve and love others abound in your everyday life. And only you can do it. You have a special way of serving that is unique to you for this time and your circle of influence.

———————

Armed with a burning heart and a combination of talents only you possess, you must now work on overcoming the obstacles in your own head. Let's target the most common issues one by one.

First up, black and white thinking. A sociologist did a fascinating study on people's reactions to litter. He put flyers on cars outside in a public place. In one scenario, he placed wadded up, flyers all around the surrounding area. In another, there was no trash anywhere, and in the third, there were just a few pieces. People were least likely to throw their flyer on the ground in the third scenario. It seems that when there was too much trash around, their actions did not seem to matter. With no trash around, they felt it would not be noticed. With just a few pieces, they were reminded of the effects of littering and felt convicted not to add to it. How often do we see so much need around us that we become overwhelmed, deciding that "if I cannot help everyone, then nothing I can do matters."

This is black and white thinking. All or none. It is, without a doubt, one of the most common barriers to overcome. If one partner "fails" to meet the expectations of the other, it can appear as if the whole relationship is ruined. It harms health. If you miss going to the gym one day, there is no need to go for the rest of the week. Eating one cookie means the entire day is blown and you might as well eat the entire box. These thoughts can go on and on, each adding to the shame of the last "failure" and blocking the next opportunity for success.

To overcome black and white thinking, we must force ourselves to find the kernel of good. Look for the areas in which you CAN help. There's an old story of an old man who saw a child throwing starfish into the ocean. He asked the boy why he was doing this. The boy answered, "The tide has washed them up onto the beach, and they can't return to the sea by themselves. When the sun gets high, they will die, unless I throw them back into the water." The old man replied, "There must be tens of thousands of starfish on this beach. I'm afraid you won't be able to make much of a difference." The boy bent down, picked up yet another starfish, and threw it as far as he could into the ocean. Then he turned, smiled, and said, "It made a difference to that one!" (adapted from The Star Thrower, by Loren Eiseley).

You may not end world hunger, but you might be someone's answer to prayer for lunch on a Tuesday. In one of my all-time favorite examples of divine appointment, a young man came into my office on his birthday. I was doing contract work with the VA, and he had been randomly scheduled with me for re-evaluation. He initially seemed defensive, coming in with stacks of files to prove his point. After I listened to his story, however, I saw his true need and began to share resources with him that I thought would be helpful. He softened and began to weep, saying that he had planned to kill himself later that day, but meeting with me had given him hope. I was doing my job. I had no way of knowing the dire state this young man was in until after I had chosen to see past his rough exterior. Your well-timed act of kindness might be what gives a hurting person the strength to make it through another day. And what an honor to play that role in the life of another! Reprogramming our minds takes time, but with repeated practice, we can learn to find the grey in a black-and-white world, and then add some color!

Next up on the list of things that hinder us: that feeling of being not good enough. This is different than the "not enoughs" we mentioned earlier. This is the feeling that I am not good enough to help anyone else. We're talking more self-shaming here in this one. The Bible provides countless examples of awful people that God used to do amazing things. David, who was called a "man after God's own heart," had his most loyal soldier killed so that he could steal his wife. Classy guy. Rahab, a prostitute, helped hide two spies sent by God AND was then listed in the genealogy of Jesus (Joshua 2; Matthew 1:5). Another prostitute anointed Jesus' feet with oil, and He replied that she would be remembered for her act of love for Him. Notice He didn't tell her that she would forever be remembered for the number of men she slept with. That wasn't what mattered to Him. And when we speak of her today, we speak of her not for her failures, but with honor, as a woman who did exactly what she was meant to do.

Let me roll this one out for you — none of us are that great. I have a tattoo with many Bible verses, one of which is Isaiah 64:6, "All of our righteous deeds are like filthy rags." Not usually one you stitch on a pillow for a graduation gift, but yet for me it has been of such great comfort. On my BEST day, when I think I am doing amazing things, being a wonderful person and nailing this whole life thing…God doesn't love me more than he did yesterday when I was rolling my eyes in the Chick Fil A line because God's waffle fries apparently take a long time to make. I believe He wants us to be and do our best for Him, which He will honor. However, He doesn't love me one ounce more when I am winning humanitarian awards than when I feel like the scum of the earth. He LOVES you. That's worth repeating. Exactly where you are right now, at this moment, He LOVES you. Just as you are, and you can go live in a camp with lepers, and He won't love you one bit more than He does when you are sitting on your couch binge-watching Netflix with a tub of Ben and Jerry's. He LOVES you. You are good enough. You will always be good enough for Him. And hear this: you always have been!

That feeling of not being good enough is generally accompanied by the added blow of thinking, "I can't even help myself." Let me tell you that it is a total lie that you have to be put together and "fixed" in order to help someone else. Most often, it is when we are in the midst of our own battles that we can recognize others in the fight. It was only in the heart of my depression that I learned to hear others cry, as well. When someone would say "I have kinda been struggling lately" in the most timid and self-minimizing tone, I began to realize that they were only sharing the tip of their iceberg, as most of us do. Below it lay miles of frozen tears weighing down their soul.

Ralph Waldo Emerson said, "It is one of the most beautiful compensations of this life, that no man can sincerely try to help another without helping himself." Alcoholics Anonymous is built on the principle that we grow as we help others. Any alcoholic will tell you that their sobriety often rests on helping others remain sober as well. I don't need to be perfect or have all the answers to begin putting into practice what I have learned. I just need to be willing to share it with an open heart. I found that the more I opened up about my own issues, the more people were able to relate to me and the more connected I felt. If I am starting on Day 1 and you are already on Day 2 of the journey, then you have something to offer.

Let me be clear. This does not mean that your purpose MUST lie in your pain. Nor does it mean that the place of your pain is the place which you are called to do the most good.

Working with eating disorders for many years, I saw two routes of recovery. In one, people would become advocates: literally getting the tattoo (a purple symbol of recovery), participating in fundraising walks and often returning to the center to speak to current patients. Recovery became integrated into their identity. Others would leave and never return again. Recovery was a battle hardfought, and once victory was established, they were off to do other things, rarely talking about it again. Neither road is superior; they are just different. Based on your own heart and talents, you can decide what to do with the newfound freedom you find when you embrace your true worth.

It's time to get up. You only need to find your path, not anyone else's. Put both feet on the ground and take a step towards what you were meant to do. Just one step, make a phone call. Research opportunities write down your vision. Just take one step. That's all you need to do today in order to guarantee you are in a different place tomorrow.

"He who has a why to live for can bear almost any how."
~ Friedrich Nietzsche

CHAPTER 4: MIND THE RIGHT GAP

———◆———

THE CLASSIC TV SITCOM SURPRISE party episode usually includes a dramatic scene with the main character crying because no one remembered her birthday…then SURPRISE! She walks into a room filled with all of her friends and family and suddenly feels extremely loved. The ironic part is that nothing changed in the ten minutes between the tears and the big reveal except the scenery and her awareness of the real situation.

Maybe sometimes you feel like your life is one of the "before" moments of the surprise party scene —as if you might be one of those people who they find three months after they died only because the postman gave up on stuffing the mail in your overflowing box. I think we all have those days. It's easy to get caught up in the idea that we don't matter to anyone else. Once that seed is planted in our brains, it begins to take root and grow.

As that seed of feeling inconsequential to the world around you grows, it chokes out your purpose. The reality is that purpose is inherently always connected to others. It is hard to feel like my life matters if I am alone on a deserted island. I am quite certain this is why Tom Hanks made Wilson on Castaway, and Will Smith greeted mannequins daily in I am Legend. We are built for connection. Relationships not only supply companionship but give us an outlet in which to practice our purpose and make meaning of our experiences in life — even the painful ones. However, problems arise when we begin to embrace the idea that our experiences are purely painful and have no value to ourselves or anyone else. And therefore, neither do we.

There is a concept in social psychology called the "confirmation bias." It states that we look for supporting evidence to prove ourselves correct, regardless of whether our premise is positive or negative. We would rather be "right" than be "good." Think about that red light that is always extra-long whenever you are running late. Guess what? It isn't. It never changes. When you are late, you notice the delay more. When we have embraced the idea that we are alone or that no one truly cares or understands us, we look for evidence to back up that thought. We notice every text that doesn't receive a reply, every meeting that gets rescheduled, and every phone call that gets cut short. Thanks to the wonders of social media, we can access pictures of every event that we are not a part of and read every comment just for our own personal torture. Thus, the evidence log of our own perceived inadequacy grows exponentially with just a few clicks. What we miss in this process is that we are proving a lie. Let's call it what it is. Making us feel isolated and alone is one of the biggest tricks of the Enemy to keep us feeling defeated in this world. We are relational beings meant to live in communion with others; even the most introverted of us all require some degree of relationship. Just ask Alexa. Many homes now include a robotic voice that can tell jokes, play games and answer your deepest questions, like "What's the difference between Under Pressure and Ice Ice Baby?" Our craving for interaction is innate and cannot be unlearned in isolation.

It is time for a plot twist. It is time to change our brains and begin to look for evidence that we ARE loved and cared for. Get up, put on some real pants, and get ready for your surprise party! It's going to be one you will never forget!

First up, we have to make sure we are correctly defining what it is that we are lacking. We have a tendency to make sweeping, global assumptions when we could instead pinpoint a particular cause with a little effort and self-reflection. Just as we discussed the importance of finishing the sentence, "I can't go one more day ….," it is important to fill in the blank of exactly who doesn't care about you that is causing this void in your life. My guess the answer is not literally "no one."

Life is all about perspective. My feeling of being loved shifts dramatically depending on what I am doing and who I am with. If I am around people doing ooey-gooey couple things, I can easily feel a sense of lacking that if I am single. As I begin to crave romantic companionship desperately, I forget to appreciate the love of friends around me that I DO have. On the other hand, my sister has an incredible family of 7 children and a loving husband. I look at her life and think she must never be lonely. Yet, she is. She desperately wants a best friend that she can depend on for playdates, margaritas, and weekend trips with the family. The idea is that there are many different relational slots in our lives that need filling, but just because one isn't filled, it does not mean that others are not. My guess is that when you feel as if no one cares, it is probably better stated as "the ONE(s) I want to care, don't care."

Identifying the exact relationship that is lacking in your life can open up your mind to appreciate the relationships that you do have. There is a story about a woman who had dreamt her entire life about going to Paris. She would picture herself in front of the Eiffel Tower, eating croissants and taking in the opulence around her. Finally, the day came for her to take her dream trip. She packed, had her itinerary planned, and boarded the plane with glee. Then it landed in Kansas. She got off the plane with a sense of shock as she looked around and saw flat plains for miles and miles. There were no fancy pastries — no golden sculptures lining the streets. And there was definitely not an Eiffel Tower. She was heartsick.

Maybe you have dreamt of a life in Paris. Your Paris might be a marriage filled with romantic gestures.

It might be a house full of children. It could be a close relationship with your own parents or siblings or a tight-knit group of friends. Whatever it is, waking up in Kansas is never fun when you expected Paris. It can seem like a raging disappointment that makes you want to cry and pout in a corner because "this isn't how it was supposed to be!" I get it. We all have an idea of how things were supposed to be. The reality is that we must learn to appreciate Kansas because we might not experience Paris as planned. With BBQ, sunflowers as big as your face, and mile after gorgeous mile of flat prairie lands…there is value in Kansas if you know where to look.

A few years ago, I lost someone that I loved very much. The stupidest things became gut punches to my emotional core. He loved pasta and would often cook for me. Truth be told, I don't even like pasta. But in the fantasy life that we dreamt of, I was going to be a noodle loving femmina. Now, I find myself angrily walking down the pasta aisle as the memories splatter over my mind like a big ole bowl of marinara sauce on a white shirt. For a brief moment, all I really want to do is sit down and scream. And maybe throw some noodles. That sounds cathartic. However, I have a choice. I can lean into the grief and wail, and rage against the fettuccini or I can take a breath and keep walking to the brownie aisle where all great things begin. Sometimes it is good to get it out. Quite frankly, I hope one day you read about a crazy lady who was found in a pile of gluten free spirals. But, in general, falling apart with a box of lasagna in my lap won't help bring him back home for dinner or help me achieve my goal of moving forward. Instead, I choose to accept my new reality of life as it is and take the next step. After all, even Paris isn't known for great spaghetti.

We all hold ideals that seem to fall short in reality. The acceptance of those "losses" can be just as painful as actual death. To help with this process, I have my clients do an exercise in which they write a eulogy grieving the loss of someone they wanted but never had. Maybe you always wanted a nurturing mother who would hug you when you fell and assure you that it would be okay, but that is NOT what you ended up with. It is okay to grieve that. It is okay to grieve the loss of your ideal childhood with married parents, your dreams of having your own child, your ideal partner, or your non-Honor Student child who just can't get it all together. Though there's nothing to bury, a hole still remains where we imagined how those relationships would look. When we accept the loss of our imaginary ideals, we can begin to appreciate people for who they are to us.

I always wanted my mom to be head of the PTA, go overboard in helping me plan my wedding and jump for joy when I called with good news. Instead, she was very introverted and quiet. VERY. Though I am sure she was proud of me, she was just not a "jumper." As long as I looked to her for these things, I felt a void. Like looking for water in a dry well, I was always thirsty. One day, as I was describing my mother to a mentor, she said, "well, that is why you are so outgoing! Your mother gave you the space to be seen and heard and be the center of attention. She let you have the floor." This observation changed my whole perspective. I began to appreciate her for what she DID provide instead of always feeling bankrupt for what she did NOT. Instead of a loss, her lack of enthusiasm started to look more like an open door for my exuberance for life. I don't take anything away from the losses you have experienced- of real things and ideals. You have to remember that your patin is never wasted or without a space to make meaning. Take some time to write your own eulogy for an ideal that does not exist. Allow yourself to acknowledge the grief of lacking. Then let the healing process begin.

———◆———

Continuing in our search for meaning, we cannot ignore the power of a self-fulfilling prophecy. A self-fulfilling prophecy is a prediction that inadvertently causes itself to become true. In this case, as I sit and think thoughts that 'no one understands me' or 'no one cares' then I begin to avoid people more and more. As I avoid them, people tend to drop communication with me. One night, I was really struggling and just wanted to hide in my covers and not talk to anyone. I had nothing to offer, and every notification on my phone was a reminder that someone else needed something from me that I could not give. Remembering this concept, I began to thank God for every ding. Each one was a symbol of someone who loved me or a job in which I was blessed to have responsibilities. This tiny act actually brought a smile to my crying face. How many times have you been feeling down and seen a text message or phone call and thought, "I don't feel like talking right now…"? After so long, the phone eventually will go quiet. Then, we sit back, lonely but proven right that truly "no one cares." It is so because we made it so with the power of the self-fulfilling prophecy.

Additionally, when we feel detached from others, we tend to hold back and not connect to those around us. If we do miraculously drag ourselves out to the gathering, we sit in a corner or quietly observe with envy while others around us seem to laugh and interact effortlessly. There's a parable of a man who wanted friends but always felt that no one liked him. After many months of working with his therapist, the therapist felt confident the man was ready to go out and make friends. She sent him on assignment to go to a party and engage with others. The man came back very disappointed. The therapist was shocked to hear how poorly it had gone. She asked the man to explain what happened. He began, "Well, I did just as you said. I put on all of my armor and grabbed my sword and sat in the middle of the room and waited for people to talk to me. They all looked afraid and went the other direction."

How often do we go to the party with our guard up and sword in hand? Then we wonder why others are put off by it. In recent times, we have finally named the look that we have all seen so many times: Resting B!$&★ Face (RBF). It's a look that says, "don't come near me." And y' all, people won't. We subconsciously evaluate others to determine their "social safety" before approaching them. Unfortunately, anxious or sad can often look like RBF, causing others to identify you as unsafe with which to interact. Research shows that tiny changes in facial expressions, such as raising one's eyebrows and giving a half-smile (you don't need a fake big-tooth clown-like grin) make others view you as more approachable.

I myself have struggled with RBF. Apparently, my "focused face" is intense. I had three different professors in college stop class and said, "Kasi, are you mad about something?" Nope. I was just intently listening. You and I both know this is NOT a good look for a psychologist to have. Can you imagine pouring your heart out to someone who looks like they would like to cut you and kick your dog? I wouldn't be too successful. I have made a genuine effort to be aware of, and consequently change, my facial expressions. I make sure to try to smile with my eyes, raise the corners of my lips slightly and nod my head a lot when I am listening to someone. It has made a world of difference.

On the other end of the spectrum of RBF is the mask of "I'm fine." A smile and "I'm fine" can make a tougher barrier to overcome than the Berlin Wall in connecting to those around us. It translates to, "I am not letting you into my world." I am not suggesting you give an honest answer to the cashier at Target who asks, "how are you doing today?" We all know her question is just part of a polite social script. However, most people in your life really do want to know. Simple questions lay the foundation of healthy relationships. It is what takes friendships to a deeper level. When it comes to feeling a sense of connection to those around us, we usually end up shooting ourselves in the foot by not being open to showing our true selves to others.

Being vulnerable is scary. We risk opening ourselves up to the potential criticism of others as well as the potential that they might fall short of our expectations and leave us disappointed. The problem is that as long as we are saying I am "fine" but really are not "fine," we don't let anyone know the real us. And then we feel like no one knows who we really are, so we disconnect further. And so continues the cycle of the self-fulfilling prophecy. And, let's be real, you don't fake it as well as you think you do. What you end up doing is avoiding building connections with others.

Building relationships takes work. We typically all have a certain number of points for the day. Work takes points. Engaging with others takes points. Every task and interaction requires a certain number of points. The problem is that things like depression, anxiety, grief, etc…are super point suckers. They make even the simplest of tasks require an exorbitant number of points to accomplish. A conversation takes points. Work takes points. Crap, sometimes breathing takes points. During a time when I was particularly struggling, I knew I had a limit on hanging out with other people before my points would run out. I could be happy and laugh for a good couple of hours before I would simply run out of the necessary amount of points required to remain "people-y." The plummet to zero was a sudden one. Like Cinderella who knew her magic would expire at midnight, I could almost feel the tears welling up inside of me, forcing me to run home, leaving behind confused friends instead of glass slippers.

One day, I had plans with a good friend of mine, but my life bars ran out before we could meet. So I made up an excuse about having to go home because I had bought fish to cook for dinner (If you know me, you know I don't cook, so that was just ridiculous). My friend rightfully got upset with me and told me that he had rearranged his whole evening to hang out with me and that I "always flake." Faced with losing a good friend that I knew I truly needed, I called and let it all out. When I finally share, it tends to come out in a higher pitch tone, rapid-fire style, in one looooooonnnggg spurt, so I don't lose the nerve to say it. I told him in one epic run-on sentence: that I had literally being crying in my car as I drove home and all I wanted to do was go home and find a suitable hole to crawl into as I had done for the past few weeks and that I couldn't handle being around people for very long, I was sorry, and it wasn't him, but I have just been struggling, and I didn't have any more points left for the day. He replied with a simple, "get your fish and come over. We can make dinner and be miserable together."

And just like that, I wasn't alone. Points didn't matter at that moment. Someone cared. Instantly, I realized that I had been hurting badly, and no one knew. After that, I decided I was on a mission to be real with the people I considered to be my closest friends. My world began to change. I felt more connected to the people around me- and they felt more connected to me. I felt safer. When friends knew I would be alone, they would ask me to come over. Almost insist. Now I had somewhere I could go when the walls started to close in. Amazingly, the walls began to expand, which meant my need for a place to run away lessened. It is truly an amazing thing that as we illuminate our darkest parts, the light begins to overtake the darkness.

One of the greatest benefits of being a psychologist is that it allows me to see that we all have a back story. My clients have friends, jobs, children, partners, and interact in the world on a daily basis. Yet, I know their hurts. I know their struggles. I know that they go home early from their high-paying job to binge and purge. I know that they leave the party early because they are too self-conscious to enjoy it. I know that they make jokes in the crowd while secretly wanting to die. We all have a back story. We all have struggles, yet don't know about them because we don't talk about them. What if we did? What if we began to open up and give ourselves permission to say, "I'm not okay." My guess is that we would all begin to realize that most of us aren't always okay.

Here is my gift to you: It is okay not to be okay. It doesn't mean that you won't always be okay. It doesn't mean that nothing is okay. No one ever said you had to have it all together to have a purpose. Life is messy. And like toddlers in a pile of mud, it is much more fun if we all get messy together and make mud pies. Someone cares. You won't lay unnoticed in a pile of your own unopened mail. I promise. You have to give those around you a chance to care. Stop avoiding people. Answer the phone. Agree to have coffee with someone new. Reach out. Share your struggles. Invite them into your mess. Eat some fish and make a mud pie.

"The grass is greener where you water it."
~ Neil Barringham

CHAPTER 5: FEELING THE LOVE

I HAVE NO SHAME IN PLANNING my own birthday parties. I do it every year. And I force my son to get just as excited about my birthday as I do his. We spend days talking about what I want to do that day and what special treat we will get to celebrate. And, when I am on my A-game, I force him to take a dollar or two of his own money and buy me a present. I usually make this announcement in third-person, so it sounds better: "We are going to the store, and you are going to use $2 and buy your mother a gift." This way, I can act surprised. Kidding. Kind of.

If this feels selfish to you, let me say there ain't nothing wrong with some love of self. We throw enough darts at ourselves that practicing some kindness and celebration is more than warranted. My former youth pastor told me that he kept a "love file" that contained cards, encouraging notes, etc., that he had received. When he was feeling unloved, he would pull it out and read them. This is brilliant, y' all. We often don't treasure the good moments enough.

Every year, I take all of the birthday cards I get,

including the preprinted one from my dentist, and I sit them on the counter for the week before and after my birthday. I keep the special ones that are particularly encouraging to me. I have cards saved from when I was a little girl that I can look back on when I feel unloved, unseen, and unheard.

When most of us think of the word, "trauma," we think something bad happened…as in your whole village was burned or you were raised in a jungle and had to forage for food, fighting gorillas with your bare hands. Anything less than that, we have a tendency to underestimate as not being "that big of a deal." The reality is that most of us have had some trauma in our lives, and we didn't label it as such. Being left at soccer practice repeatedly can send a message that you don't matter if you were constantly overlooked by teachers or coaches, its easy to feel unseen. And it takes very few instances of being told to just "deal with it" to feel unheard. These are all forms of trauma. Any of which can cause wounds to our hearts and minds that will undoubtedly influence the way we view ourselves. The good news is that, in the same way, we received negative messages, we can find healing as we send positive messages to ourselves about who we really are.

We send messages to ourselves every day in everything that we do. Every time you choose to do something nice for yourself, you are subtly whispering "I am worth it" to the depths of your heart. After a while, those whispers will begin to drown out the biting digs that say you are not good enough. You must learn to be gentle with yourself. You are God's creation, an intricate being made in His image.

I am well aware that, unfortunately, many people have not had a positive experience with God. Maybe you think you have seen God in the form of a distant father, a critical mother, or a hyper-critical pastor. While I am not going to take time here to go deep into who HE is, let me say that He is none of those. He has the unfortunate "gift" of being represented by people who are no representation of Him at all. The real God loved you so much that He died for you (John 3:16). He longs to heal you. He not only hears your cries, but your tears are so precious to Him that He bottles them (Isaiah 56:8). I envision this shelf with your name on it, filled with bottles, each labeled with a different hurt from your life: that horrible breakup, the fight with your mother, the moment you were left behind, the day you lost your best friend. Imagine the love and proximity required to bottle someone's tears. It is mind-blowing. I pray you to experience the real God, the one who loves you so much that your name is inscribed on His hand (Isaiah 49:6). As we learn to receive His love fully, we can begin to love ourselves.

If we are going to find our place in the world… to find our purpose, we must first learn to love ourselves and receive love from other people. The purpose is all about connection to one another. If I don't feel loved, then connection starts to feel meaningless at best and unsafe at worst. Nothing says "rejected" like holding a hand up to high five someone, and they leave you hanging. When we aren't able to receive love, we are asking someone to high five a hand so far out of reach; they could never jump high enough to touch it. It doesn't matter how hard someone tries to love you if you have buried your heart so deep that it cannot be reached.

Why is it so hard to receive love? To allow someone else to love you fully? Sometimes we feel unworthy of ANY love. When we don't see what's special about ourselves, we struggle to understand how or WHY another person might love us. They might profess their love, but if it doesn't make sense, then we cannot receive it. What if I called you today and told you that you won a raffle and I would be bringing you a new car? All you had to do was show up to receive it. If you hadn't bought a raffle ticket, you probably would not believe me, so you would not even try to get the car. In much the same way, we see the love of others as winning a prize that we didn't earn, much less deserve.

I spend most of my days trying to help people learn skills to make their lives better, whether it's how to make peace with food to overcome eating issues or resolving stuck points of a trauma that haunts them. The theme I most frequently hear, no matter what the struggle, is that they do not feel they are worth it. They don't feel worthy of treating their body with gentle care and feeding it nourishing meals three times per day. They don't feel worthy of being set free from the scars left by another.

They don't feel worthy of loving themselves and demanding that others treat them lovingly. I can teach them all the skills and tools and tricks in the world, but if they don't love themselves and feel worthy of that love, then they won't do any of it. And neither will you.

Have you ever seen a dirty Porsche? Think about it. They are always spotlessly clean and unblemished. You will never see a Porsche with a scratch in the paint that goes unrepaired. Why? Because someone who owns a Porsche most likely loves their car. They know the value of it. They know what it's worth. On the flip side, my first car was a 1989 brown Ford Taurus (if you don't know this car, imagine a giant refrigerator box with four doors… it was sexy). I probably washed it three times in the first year I had it. I hoped the dust would make it look grey since I hate the color brown. I once got lightly rear-ended at a red light and just told the guy not to worry about it. A few scratches on the bumper wasn't going to make that car any worse.

Taking care of yourself requires investing time, energy, and resources into you. Until you know your worth, you won't love yourself enough to invest in yourself. It is almost impossible to realize your worth if you are walking around with a clearance sticker on your forehead and treating yourself accordingly.

How often have I heard a woman say that she doesn't know the last time she moisturized her face. Y'all, this is a little thing, but come on. You are worth a jar of night cream and the 30 seconds it takes to put it on. You are worth getting the entree you want on the menu and not the cheapest thing. Don't always look at the right side of the menu where the prices are first. Pick out what you want. You are worth taking $60 and an hour for a massage. You are worth THOSE shoes.

One year, I was hosting a New Year's party that required everyone to wear cocktail attire. I was so excited to buy a new dress. I went to Filene's Bargain Basement, shopping the clearance racks. I finally found a dress with a stain on it that I thought would get me an extra discount off the already reduced price of $27. Thankfully, my husband, at the time, drew the line and declared that I was worth more than a dirty dress! I argued that I didn't care about that and we needed to save money. I never thought I was worth spending some of our family money on things for me. He came up with a wonderful idea to give me a designated amount of money each month for the "Kasi fund." The only rule was that I HAD to spend it on myself, whether I saved many months for a big-ticket item or bought something smaller each month...I had to use it just for me. As trivial as this sounds, that was a huge shift in learning to appreciate the value of self-care! I had to practice loving on myself and valuing my wants each time I spent that money.

I wish I could snap my fingers and take away all of your dirty dresses and make you feel worthy of splurging. Whether it is on an amazing pair of shoes or a girlfriend who treats you with respect, I wish you could see that you are worth it all. I wish I could magically show you who you really are instead of you only seeing the lies that you have believed for so long. I can tell you a good place to start. Let's take a look at who the Creator of the Earth says you are. He made you, and it is inevitable that He made you with intent and sees value in you.

The Bible is filled with messages about who you really are. One year, I read the entire Bible with the intent of writing down every verse I could find that tells me who God says I am. The list is in the appendix, but I highly recommend doing such a study for yourself. As you make a point to SEARCH for your identity in the right places actively, you will be amazed at what you find. You are a garden of his delight (Isaiah 5:7), clothed with strength and dignity (Proverbs 31:25), the apple of His eye (Psalm 119), God's friend (James 2:23), close to God's heart (Psalm 48:14), complete in Christ (Colossians 2:10), crowned with glory and honor (Psalm 8:5), washed, sanctified and justified (I Cor 6:1), and God's own treasured possession (Psalm 135:4). Read that list again and let it sink into your soul. Let its message drown out the voice in your head that says that you are not enough. Pick a few that stand out to you most and write your own identity statement. Write it on your bathroom mirror. Make it the wallpaper on your phone. Memorize it. Repeat it every day until you believe it in your very core.

When we give ourselves unconditional love,

we discover the conditions under which we felt unloved. Remember that we just talked about the importance of those little messages that we send ourselves to say that we are loved. The sad reality is that we have most likely received messages from others, too, saying that we aren't. When someone professes to love you but does not treat you in a loving manner, you have to either redefine what love is or accept that they don't love you. Sadly, it is often easier to redefine love than to make that leap of acceptance.

I was in a very toxic relationship for several years. Even though I knew that he was breaking me more every minute that we were together, I could not let him go because he said that he "loved" me. If you have ever been "loved" by someone toxic, whether it is a partner, a parent, or a friend, you know that it can set the mind spinning. His "love" meant calling me selfish regularly and leaving me crying when I did not do exactly what he wanted. His "love" required me to give him my body any time he wanted it, in any way that he wanted it. He would see my tears and not blink, yet he continued to point out how much he "loved" me. In spite of all this, I consistently forced myself to remember the shred of good that we had or the few nice things he had done. This was not hard because after all, even a broken clock is right twice a day. Few things are ever completely bad. But when the bad outweighs the good, it's time to go. There are a million things that led to my finally being able to walk away with peace, but the most memora-ble was when I found a bracelet he had given me on our anniversary. I realize that I could take the good that I thought was there with me and leave behind the bad. I didn't have to get rid of all of it and pretend it never happened. I could keep the bracelet as a symbol of the positive lessons that I learned from it and walk away from all the hurt. After I found the courage to walk away, I began to see how bad it really was. And how much better I deserve. Today, I wear that bracelet almost every day - not to remember him- but to honor my choice to be treated better.

It may take time before you see the impact that someone else's toxicity had in your life. At first, it may just feel like a loss. Slowly, you will begin to sift reality from manipulation. Similar to watching the movie Sixth Sense, and that moment when you realize that he was really a ghost. Afterward, you begin to replay the whole movie in your head. Suddenly, you can't NOT see it in every scene. Distance allows truth to be revealed and shine its light on every dark memory.

I was very far removed from him before I could see that he did not love me at all. He just wanted to own me. When I would push away and try to leave, he chased me not out of love, but as a child clings to a toy, he does not want but doesn't want anyone else to have. When you allow someone to treat you poorly, it says more about your own love of self than it does their love for you. I struggled for so long to leave thinking I loved him, and he could change…but really I struggled because I didn't love myself enough to demand better. I didn't know what love was; therefore, I had let him define it for me in a way that was grossly inaccurate. While this was a painful realization, it set me free to define- and then find- actual love and to love myself.

Friendships, siblings, and parents can all be toxic. Unfortunately, part of the toxicity is the hold that they have on us, which makes it difficult to leave. When I don't love myself, and I don't know my worth, I have no standard for how others should treat me. Most often, the toxic outside voice is only echoing the nasty voices in our own head, so we find it difficult to argue with. Instead, we hang our heads in defeat and wonder what it would feel like to be loved, assuming we must just be UNLOVE-ABLE. I'm not letting toxic people off the hook by any means, but the reality is that change has to start with me. I have to love who I am before I can ever expect someone else to love me. Otherwise, it's like trying to fill a jug of water without the hole on the bottom being plugged. It will all just spill back out and never make it where it was meant to be.

To truly love yourself, you have to stop running your pain. When I get stressed, or something bad happens, my first instinct is to run away. I am the type to buy a same-day plane ticket and escape. The reality is that no matter what destination I pick, whenever I get there…I would still be there. I cannot run away from me; try as I might. And I have tried. We have all tried. Maybe you tried to escape for a week by going on vacation. Maybe you tried to escape for a weekend by drinking copious amount of alcohol. Maybe you have filled your closet with enough shoes to support a centi-pede. Maybe you get lost in a box of donuts. Maybe you tried to escape for a night by taking sleeping pills and ending the day early. No matter how or for how long, we have all run away at some point.

One of the hardest things I teach my clients to do is to sit with themselves. It is absolutely frighten-ing to most people. That's why we drown out our own voice with the constant hum of a TV, a nev-er-ending to-do list, and people who are less than healthy for us. Think about all the things you do to avoid just sitting and being with yourself. When is the last time you drove in silence? Is that hard for you? Why is it so hard to sit with yourself without listing your faults like you were looking to cause an earthquake big enough to knock off California? Why can't you be at peace with who you are in this moment?

Sometimes we are afraid of what we will find if we sit quietly and look inside ourselves. Fun fact: Babies are only born with the fear of two things: falling and loud noises. That's it. Everything else is learned. If you've ever struggled with depression, anxiety, trauma, or quite simply just being human, it likely made a mark on you that left you wanting never to feel that way again. Thus we develop a fear of our own emotions. We learn creative ways to avoid ourselves in order to deal with our fear.

As humans, we are hard-wired to respond to fear of any kind with avoidance. The most ironic-kick-in-the-pants part of fear is that it is self-reinforcing.

What that means is this: Let's say I am afraid of spiders. I believe that if I get within a few feet of a spider, it will somehow leap across the room, bite me, and ultimately kill me. I avoid spiders at all costs. And guess what?! I don't get bit, and I don't die. I learn that my avoidance works! It keeps me safe, which means I keep doing it. And the more I do it, the more the horrible consequence doesn't happen, so I keep doing it. And after a certain period of time, I am completely convinced (even if it is on a subconscious level) that my fear has kept me safe.

The real kicker is that fear can never be ordered a la carte. It is always served on a buffet table with avoidance of relationships or activities, anxiety, and a side of self-doubt. Fear is also a parasite. It feeds on our need for security and connection. It consumes our thoughts, time, and energy as it requires increasing effort to keep at bay. I must think about the consequences and find an alternative plan that is less likely to cause me pain. In all of this, I have little left to devote to finding my purpose. My focus shifts inward on maintaining my own safety, rather than outward on expressing the talents I have been given.

The real problem comes when we believe that WE are poisonous. That our own emotions will kill us if we begin to dive into them. I went through a period of horrible depression in college, which left me living in fear and dread of that ever happening again. I kept myself busy. I worked almost full-time while earning my doctorate degree. I surrounded myself with people every moment I wasn't at work or in school. Sometimes the unexpected would still happen and crash my fragile house of cards. For example, I was coasting along being busy one day when my then-husband found out he would have to go on a work trip for two weeks. Panic rushed over my body. Where would I go? What would I do? We had just moved to a new city, and I did not have many friends. Two weeks alone sounded horrific. I could not fathom how I would survive. I booked plane tickets that same day to fly home and visit my family in Texas. Those tickets brought a sense of relief, but also a sense of sadness that I couldn't just stay at home alone like a "normal" person.

What do you do when that panic rushes over you? Do you keep it at bay by constantly surfing Facebook, binge-watching Netflix, or keeping a steady diet of HGTV? Avoiding the sound of your own voice requires more noise than any Pandora station can ever generate.

While my self-avoidance did improve over time, I still found myself just "managing" my fears, rather than conquering them. I would tell clients to practice sitting in the quiet for three minutes at a time and work their way up to 20, but no way on earth was I going to try it. I was afraid of what I might find in those moments. Admittedly, I don't know that sitting with yourself is a drug to which you slowly build tolerance, enabling you to take it in larger doses. Rather, I think it is part of a process that comes with making peace with yourself.

EVERY piece of you. Accepting yourself for who you are, just as you are, right where you are. You don't have to hurry up and get over it, figure it out, or get it done. You can take your time. You can just be for a minute. With this permission, your mind begins to feel less like a monster hiding under the bed and more like a friend that you can sit in silence with and not feel the need to speak. The friends that don't require words are your real friends, anyways.

Let me help you begin to check the facts about your fear: You are not a Pandora's box of pain that can never be shut once it is opened. If you allow yourself to feel love, you won't be exposed to heartache beyond comprehension. If you acknowledge your past hurts, they will stop tainting your present. I promise if you start crying, you will be able to stop. In fact, crying can be one of the most healing things you can do for your entire body. Natural tears (like from looking at a bright light) are made of 98% water. Emotional tears are mostly made of cortisol. Cortisol is the hormone released in response to stress as part of the fight-flight-freeze mechanism. Elevated cortisol levels interfere with learning and memory, lower immune function and bone density, and increase blood pressure, cholesterol, and heart disease, among many other things. It is known to make depression worse and even lower life expectancy. In other words, you want it out. Crying is the body's natural release valve for cortisol. This is why you usually really do feel better after a good cry.

Put another way: You are made up of ALL of you. Your tears, your joy, your depression, your fears, your love for others, your dreams, your setbacks. All of it. You cannot choose the parts you accept and the parts you hide like you're an a la cart buffet. It's a package deal. The peas come with the steak. No substitutions.

You must stop running from yourself. Stop. Take a moment and look inside. Truly look inside. Allow yourself to see from the eyes of another all the things that have terrified you. All your shame. Your hurts. Your loss. Your pain. Like shadows on the wall in the middle of the night, none of it is as scary in the daylight as it appears in the dark. Learn to love your "dark" parts. Make peace with all your pieces, and you will find that they don't seem so bad.

Chew on this: Out of 43,000 types of spiders in the world, less than 30 have ever been responsible for human death. Let me break that down for you: that's 0.0007%. You see, you didn't need your fear and avoidance of spiders to keep you safe from them. They were never really a danger to you, anyways. And neither are you! There is nothing inside of you to fear. Take the journey and do not be afraid to love who you really are. Love reveals everything that is unlike itself. It will highlight inconsistencies and places that have kept you stuck, freeing you up to be filled up beyond your wildest dreams.

Explore your depths. Learn to celebrate yourself.

EVERY part of yourself. You are more lovable – and loved – than you could ever know.

"I don't want everyone to like me; I should think less of myself if some people did."
~ Henry James

CHAPTER 6: THE VALUE OF FULL PRICE

FLASHBACK TO YOUR 3RD-GRADE SCI-ENCE lessons and recall that matter is anything that has mass and takes up space. Basically, it's all the stuff you can see. In the 1950s, studies of other galaxies showed that stars traveled at the same rate through identifiable matter as through black spaces that seemed to contain nothing. This proved that there must be something there, through which it was traveling, although it was unseen. Enter the term, dark matter. It emits no light or energy but has mass and takes up space. Scientists believe that 80% of the Universe is actually dark matter that we cannot see with the naked eye, yet it impacts how we view all that we can see. Dark matter is critical to the universe functioning as we know it.

Unfortunately, most of life is dark matter. You can't see it, but it's critical to life as we know it. In today's Instagram, Snapchat society, we expect life to be very public and very fast. We are constantly determining if a particular moment in our life is post-worthy...or, even just worthy. We want the overnight success, though we tend to forget how dark the night can be. The truth is, it is most often what is done in secret that is the most critical part of your day and your preparation for the next day.

The most important jobs you have will most likely begin in secret. Nursing mothers spend hours in the night with their babies without anyone around to notice — Doctors intern and train for years before they become sought-after surgeons. Ed Sheeran, whom my heart adores, gave up everything to move from the UK to LA where he busked, performing on the streets for donations, and played free open mic events. Eventually, Jamie Foxx heard him and invited him to play at his house. He is now he is one of the highest-grossing artists of all time. His talent was developed on the streets day in and day out before he became an "overnight success." I am sure that playing for free on the streets made for one very long night.

I began doing presentations and preaching in small churches long before anyone knew my name. After watching one of them, a friend shared that I had said the word, "um" 56 times. Let me, um, be the first, um to tell you that if you um had heard me then, you would not be reading this now. I had much to learn about how to speak in public. Even more importantly, I had much to learn about myself.

I needed to learn who I was and where my value really lay to ensure that I didn't waste my time performing someone else's gifts for someone else's praise. When you have confidence in something, you don't feel the need to prove it. You simply know that it is so. And, if someone questions it, you don't even have to defend yourself because you are secure in your position.

We typically don't feel the need to prove what we know to be true. There are people who don't believe the Holocaust happened, some who believe the Earth is flat, and that pineapple isn't meant for pizza. These beliefs seem so ridiculous that most of us would not bother to argue with them. Either they will eventually figure it out, or they will go through life being wrong, but you are probably not going to change their mind. When you know something to be true, you don't need to prove it. You already know it.

The same principle reigns true for how we see ourselves. The things we feel most led to perform are usually the places where we feel the most inse-cure, be it our appearance, a particular skill set, a job, or even for the approval of another. One of the greatest gifts of discovering who I am is that I am have lost much of my need to prove that I have it all together. Recently, I was headed to a semi-for-mal dinner when my dress tore as I got into the car. A normal person probably would have gone back inside to change, but not me. Nope, I just sewed that puppy up in the car and went with it. And, of course, I made sure to tell people about it, lest I come across as more put together than I really am.

Truthfully, have never been really put together. I always have hairs out of place. Somehow, my blush likes to smear in a straight line across my cheek that someone will kindly need to remind me to blend.

My clothes are usually a little wrinkled because I feel they are going to end up that way anyway after being in the car, so why waste time ironing now. Truthfully, I didn't even own an iron until two years ago when I bought one at a garage sale for $1, so my son and I could make iron-on t-shirts. I still eat the cookies covered in powdered sugar because they are my favorites, knowing full well I will look like I got caught in a snowstorm afterward. These are things that I have come to accept - and even appreciate- about myself. I don't need to have it all together. I am okay being perfectly imperfect. And life is way too short to eat a biscuit without jelly just because there is a high probability of ending up with a grape stain on my shirt.

There is a great peace that comes with realizing that no one is spotless. No one has it all together. The beauty of this human being thing does not lie in its perfection, but in its realism. We are all just making our way through life, trying not to fall down or say something ridiculous. This realization releases the pressure valve on the old performance tank, allowing you to fully embrace who you are without having to prove your abilities to anyone else.

The pressure to perform is pervasive across social and economic lines. Elvis Presley has over one billion fans today, even though he died in 1977. He is still referred to as "The King of Rock and Roll" and continues to hold the record for the most top 40 Hits (141). He is in five music hall of fames and the only person ever to be on two postage stamps. In 2015, 38 years after his death, his estate released a new album of his songs which hit #1 on charts around the world. Yet, he always questioned if it would one day be taken away and he would be left with nothing and no fame. He doubted if he would leave any legacy, feeling no one would remember him after he died. In an interview in Reader's Digest, Priscilla Presley said, "Elvis never came to terms with who he was meant to be or what his purpose in life was. There was always that question, "Was I chosen?" He thought he was here for another reason. Maybe to preach, to save, to care for people. That agonizing desire was always in him. And he knew he wasn't fulfilling it. So he'd go on stage, and he wouldn't have to think about it."

Who are you performing for? What fear are you trying to drown out by creating your own show? Who are you trying to convince that you are worthy of love, smart enough to be in your seat at work, or good enough to make a difference? I spent years trying to convince my mother I was worthy of her praise. I would call her with every new accomplishment, hoping for an exciting response or a celebratory cake. It hurts my heart to think of me- a grown, married grad student, making her a wall hanging for Christmas, and thinking, "maybe she will think I am talented…." Then I finally realized that I had her affection and pride; she just had a different way of showing it than what I was expecting. Maybe you, too, are craving the praise of a parent, or a spouse, a teacher, a supervisor or the hardest of all to please….yourself. This need to prove your worth becomes a black hole in which no amount of praise or accolades can fill. Just ask Elvis.

Whether you top Billboard charts or make charts for a classroom of students, you will not find fulfill-ment until you believe in yourself enough that you no longer have anything to prove. So how do you do that? Let's start by addressing some false beliefs that many of us hold.

Up first, is the idea that perfection is directly cor-related to lovability. Translated: "If I have enough of X quality, then people will love me." All of us tend to have a different magical quality that we hold near and dear as the golden key to total acceptance. This leads us to work to maximize our performance efforts in that category to prove that we have it. Remember when Hugh Grant cheated on Eliza-beth Hurley? How many people said, "How could he cheat on her? She is so beautiful…" There's an underlying belief to that statement which implies that someone who is beautiful should never have to deal with the pain of adultery. We do this with almost every area of life, from finances to career success and even….religiosity. One of my dear friends was married to a pastor. People frequently told her, "you are so lucky to be married to such a Godly man!"

I am not saying that these qualities aren't import-ant or have value. However, just because they have value doesn't mean that they determine YOUR value. That is the critical distinction point. You don't have to be a beauty queen, the King of Comedy, or the Goddess of Godly to be lovable. You are a beautiful conglomeration of traits, some messy and some seamless, some light and some dark, but all combined make you the lovable DNA pile that you are.

The next false belief that has to go is the idea that people admire a perfect product more than the process. I had the pleasure of watching the 5th-grade talent show at my son's school. I was so impressed by every brave child who got up to perform. One girl, in particular, got lost in the third verse of a song and missed a few lines. As soon as the chorus began again, she started to sing, and the audience went nuts applauding. I promise she was one of the most memorable performances, not because it was flawless but because she demonstrated such grace and courage as she kept going. That is my challenge to you. Take pride in the process. Embrace all of it, not just the time you nail it in the end. You will undoubtedly forget the words more times than not in life, but if you keep going, you will get back to a part you know. Let's be real; most people only know the chorus anyways.

Take some time and identify the areas you are trying to perform in your life. Write them down. Ask yourself what you are trying to prove and to who? And why? For the love of Pete, why do you have to prove anything to anyone? There is nothing wrong with striving to be better, but the need to perform in order to feel validated - or really to feel the hole in your soul- is what has to go - like now.

———•———

Conversely, maybe you have given up trying to perform because you feel, like Eeyore, as if it won't make a difference anyway. Like a big glob of dark matter floating in the galaxy, maybe you feel unseen as if your preferences don't matter. It doesn't matter which movie you want to watch. It doesn't matter what you say; people won't listen anyway. It doesn't matter what you do with your body, or to your body for that matter. It doesn't matter because you don't matter. However, just like substances invisible to the naked eye can affect the amount of light visible from a star, so you affect the amount of light that everyone around you sees. And, hear this: you also get to determine how much of your own light, you see.

How you view yourself impacts every decision that you make or don't make, from what to eat to who you spend your time with. Your view of self is the foundation on which all other relationships are built. There's nothing more discouraging than feeling as if your place in this life is inconsequential. It really knocks the fruity taste right out of fruit punch. The question is, where did that feeling come from?

I have a client who experienced some pretty severe childhood abuse. When she finally told her parents, her mother responded with anger. Her disclosure disrupted the "family system." In her words, "Her choosing her family told me I don't matter, and I developed this dialogue that I'm a burden. I'm not worth anything." The roots of your belief may not be as blatant or obvious as in this example, but I am sure that at some point in your life you still had an experience in which the message was clear:" You are hurting, but we will do nothing about it." In other words, you don't matter.

Unfortunately, once internalized, this message gets reinforced on a daily basis. For example, if I believe that no one cares about what I have to say, I will sit quietly and say nothing. If you recall from an earlier chapter, this creates what we call in "fancy" psychological terms, a "self-fulfilling prophecy." That means we make our own fate. Perhaps, instead of replaying your conversations for the judge in your head to score, we need to reconsider what is truly valuable.

If you are going to critique every word that comes from your mouth, you might as well define what is really important anyways. I don't know who you hang out with, but most of my friends are not dropping wisdom bombs on the regular. It's generally just conversation. Talking about life, love, the weather, and who has the best tacos in town. (To be fair, the taco part may be of value.) Everything else matters because the person who is saying it matters. I love my friends, and therefore, I deeply care about their thoughts even about trivial things. It's how we connect. It's how we get to know people and build a foundation for deeper relationships, one menial conversation at a time. Don't underes-

timate your value or the value of your seemingly
meaningless words. They are windows to your
world. And hear me when I say, your world is valuable.

The dictionary defines worthless as "having no
good qualities; deserving contempt." While the last
part sounds harsh, how often do we treat ourselves
as if we are truly worthless, i.e., DESERVING of
contempt? There is a skill I teach my clients called
"check the facts." Get ready for this shocker: It
means you should check the facts on your erro-
neous beliefs. Ask yourself where they came from.
WHY do you deserve contempt? What did you do
that was so incredibly awful? List facts. Not random explanations. Try to think of actual, factual
proof, as if you were in a courtroom trying to justify your beliefs.

If you begin to argue your case, you will probably find that your testimony begins in childhood.
There is something called the "critical period" for
many aspects of development in which a particular skill or characteristic is thought to be most
readily acquired. The animal world offers amazing examples of this concept. For example, ducks
must "imprint" on their mother within the first
few hours of birth. This is the time when a duck
realizes it is a duck and commits to following its
mother around and learning to be a duck. If the
mother is not around, then the duck will imprint
on the first thing that it sees. Researcher Conrad
Lorenz discovered this phenomenon and a group
of newborn ducklings imprinted on him, follow-

ing him around wherever he went.

While humans are thankfully MUCH more adaptive than ducks, there is still a point in our development where we are looking for someone to tell us who we are. Even as adults, we spend much of our lives looking for someone to show us what we are supposed to do in life. We're looking for our equivalent of a "how to be a duck" manual. What if we are taught that we are something else —something far less than what we were created to be?

As children, we are pretty powerless. We don't have control over our environment. We need someone else to provide the food we eat, give us shelter, ensure we get to school, etc. Children are at the mercy of the adults in their life. If those adults are unsafe, the entire world becomes unsafe. There is nothing any child can do about it. To cope with this reality, it is much easier for a child to take on the belief "I am bad," rather than "the people that are supposed to take care of me are bad." Taking the burden on myself gives me the illusion that I can control what happens to me. If I am good enough, then my Dad won't hit me. If I keep the house clean enough, my Mom won't yell at me. If I don't look a certain way, I won't be attractive to perpetrators of that abuse. It is quite easy to make life into a complex formula of rules and standards designed to protect me. When these standards of "good enough" do not work to keep me safe, they quickly get replaced by the need for perfect adherence to the formula. And when that doesn't work,

I am left to conclude that I am truly just worthless. I am deserving of contempt.

Let me clear something up for you. I don't know who in your life did not treat you like the precious gem that you are. I don't know what they did. I do know we are not responsible for the actions of another. You cannot cause another person to hit you, touch you inappropriately, or call you names. You are not that powerful. We all have control over how we respond to others, no matter what they do. You are not meant to bear the burden of another's actions.

It is time we take the blame off ourselves and learn to label our emotions appropriately. It is okay to be angry. Yes, the ultimate goal is to forgive. That is where true freedom lies. But how can you forgive someone of something for which you have never held them accountable? You are reducing the sentence of someone who was never even found guilty. It does not work that way. First, there must be a recognition that a wrong occurred. You were, and still are, worthy of being treated far better than you were. What happened to you is not okay. It's not "fine."

There is a law of human nature that says that when a crime, or wrongdoing, is committed, there should be a consequence. Often, if someone does not feel empowered to give consequence to the person who mistreated them, the one wronged will naturally assume the consequence. Someone must be punished for this, and I am the only one left to bear the weight of the crime, so it must be me. I then accept less than I deserve in my next relationship. I self-harm. I deny myself food. I keep a running tape in my head to remind me of how awful I am. The list goes on. Just name your own go-to form of self-punishment.

Healing comes when you realize that it is not your job to pass a sentence for the crime committed against you. That is a job far bigger than your human mind can handle. You cannot punish yourself any more than you can dole out punishment for anyone else. You are not the judge or jury. You are simply a witness. You are a carrier of truth. By bearing witness to the truth, you begin to find freedom from your own guilt and shame. And by learning to forgive, you will find freedom from your anger – both internal and external.

When anger is turned inward, it produces depression. Our response is internalizing shame, rather than accepting the reality of the situation and holding others appropriately accountable, including ourselves. It is FAR easier for me to say, "well, maybe I'm just an awful person" after I hurt someone that I love than to sit down and consider what I did and why I chose to do it. Life is about choices. Labeling myself as simply awful takes away my autonomy to choose to do better at the moment. It renders me helpless to change and to make things better.

Check the facts. Did you really do something wrong to deserve the feelings of worthlessness that you have? If not, don't continue to take the consequences of others' choices out on yourself. If you did, consider what led to those actions, rather than labeling yourself a castoff. Apologize appropriately, but just for your actions — not someone else's.

I hear the words, "I'm sorry" a lot. If someone reaches around me for something, they often say, "I'm sorry." For what? For reaching? For needing a pen? For taking up space? What are you sorry for? It seems like a tiny exercise in semantics, but practice saying "excuse me" instead. It's great to be polite, but you don't need to apologize. Apologies are for when you did something wrong. Remember that.

Not everyone apologizes. Imagine two people, Suzi and Jack. Suzi cheats on Jack while they are married. Jack packs a suitcase for her. In it, he places the loss of his self-esteem, his heartache, feelings of regret, anger, and resentment. Across the front, he scrawls "Suzi" in huge black letters. Suzi refuses to take it. She leaves it on his door and goes on to begin her new life. Jack picks up the suitcase and decides to keep it so that he never forgets the pain he felt, or who caused it. Someone must claim this baggage. Years go by, and Jack meets a beautiful young woman, Erica. But Jack can't hug Erica. He only has one arm because the other is carrying the suitcase. Soon Erica tires of one-armed hugs and walking slowly on dates to accommodate Jack and his incredibly heavy luggage and leaves. Jack is once again heartbroken and thinks of how different his life would be if only Suzi had taken the suitcase with her instead of leaving it with him to carry.

Perhaps, like Jack, you are one who needs to forgive someone who never asked for it. You have found yourself carrying reminders for someone who will not be reminded of their infractions. Forgiveness breaks down into two words: for and give. It is what you choose to give in exchange for a wrong done to you. It is a gift for yourself that you give to someone else. Choosing to forgive someone does not erase the consequences of their actions. It is not a stamp of approval for wrongs done. It does not require you to have a relationship with the person going forward. In fact, the true beauty of forgiveness is that it requires nothing of you but to lay down the burden of accountability for someone else's actions. It is freeing. Take some time and think about what you need to give for your hurts.

It's also important to ask where you find your worth. I decided to teach my son about investments. I took a little bit of money and told him that he could choose what stocks we would buy, which we could monitor over time to see how they performed. At that time, fidget spinners were all the rage. He had about ten of them, and so did every kid in his class. He suggested we buy stock in fidget spinners. I explained to him that, although they were very popular at the moment, those would be a passing craze that would soon be replaced by something else. It would not be a good place to put our money. We had to think long-term. What could we invest in that would be likely to be around for a while? Who is solving a problem that will have a lasting impact? Who is growing and developing something that will last? That is where we should invest. At the time of writing this, just a few months after that conversation, fidget spinners have already phased out. You can find them on clearance in most places. Their value has gone down significantly.

It is very easy for us to base our own value on a "passing craze." If I pass this test, I am a good person. If this person loves me, I am worth loving. If I get this job, I will know that I am good enough. The problem is that those things are fleeting. If we invest in them, we will find our value quickly drops, and we are left with a clearance sticker on our souls, offering ourselves to anyone who will take us. The pain and the rejection of this pattern are cumulative; our value drops a little more each time we put it on the market.

We must begin to define our worth not by the things of this world but by the One who created us. We are made IN THE IMAGE of a Holy GOD. Read that again. Let it sink in. You are made in the image of God Himself. You are not defined by the job you have or the partner who loves you any more than a van Gogh painting is valued by where it hangs. Your worth is intrinsic. It remains no matter where you are or what you are doing. That does not mean that you are meant to hang in a crack shack. Most van Goghs don't. But the value of it doesn't change based on the wall on which it hangs.

No matter where you have been, what you have done, or what has been done to you, it is important you realize none of that changes WHO you are, or quite frankly WHOSE you are.

I could take Starry Night all over the slums, drag it through the mud, call it a Backstreet Boys poster, and hang it upside down. The labels I put on it don't change its worth. In the end, it is still a priceless work of art painted by one of the greatest painters who ever lived.

I haven't yet made it to Van Gogh-purchasing status, but I recently bought a BMW. I have never had a car this nice. The bumper to the car I traded in for it was zip-tied in because I hit a deer and never got it fixed. Now, I find myself trying to drive a little better. I am aware of how close I park to other cars (nobody wants a door ding in a BMW). I no longer put my makeup on in my car because I don't want fingerprints of blush and eye shadow on the visor. I am changing how I do things because I don't want the same old patterns that have affected my other vehicles to mess up my new car. I want this one to be different because I know what this car is worth, not just price-wise, but what it symbolizes for me.

It is time to reappraise your life. Take off the clearance stickers that you have allowed to be stuck on you. Your worth is not in what you have done.

Your value is certainly not based on what has been done to you. Your worth is deep inside of you, as a precious child of God, created a little lower than the angels. No one can ever change that. You have value simply because you are. You will never be worth more or less than you are at this moment.

Today, you are new. When you walk into a new house, you take off your shoes so as not to drag the residue of where you have been into the house and dirty the floor. Take off your shoes right now. Stop carrying someone else's harsh words into your future. Shake off the dust of your own shame. Leave behind old judgments that will muddy your foundation. Remember that you matter, simply because you matter.

"She made broken look beautiful and strong look invincible. She walked with the Universe on her shoulders and made it look like a pair of wings."
~ Ariana Dancu

CHAPTER 7: TAKING A LEAP

I WORKED IN THE SAME CLINIC for seven years. My plan from the day I started was to take over and run it eventually. I never planned to leave. I enjoyed the stability of paid vacation days, health insurance, and a predictable salary. Then one day, ...this happened:

Yup. That's me. With all of my books, degrees, and office-ly possessions stacked in the back of my car after I was fired from the job I never planned to leave. While my ego took a sucker punch, something in me knew that day was going to end up being one of the best days of my life. I just needed a little push to move on from the plan I had made for myself to a far better plan. You see, I had built a house where God only intended for me to create a tent. And that thing had to burn down around me before I got out.

Before this day, I was miserable in my job. Ownership had changed. Leadership had changed. We weren't even allowed to have the same office furniture anymore. My comfy couch was replaced with a sterile metal chair, which was not conducive to therapy. I had no intentions of quitting. It was stable. It was predictable. Most of all, it was familiar. I knew the issues associated with it. What if I took a new job and the furniture was even worse than what I already had? A known hell is better than unknown heaven. Because the benefits of leaving were unknown, I chose to continue to pay the costs of staying because I could afford them. And I could't afford the cost of my mortgage if I left.

Most of us have a natural human tendency to build houses. We want the basic structure of life in place. We build houses in relationships that we have no business even passing through. We move into jobs that we are only meant to pass through for a season. We forward our mail to the Corner of Brokenness and Scars from the Past that was only meant to be tourist stops on our journey. All because we crave stability more than a possibility. We focus on memorizing our address instead of asking if we even like the house.

We must give ourselves permission to be more fluid. Permission to not have all the answers and all the boxes checked. You have permission to change your mind. When you were a child, you probably loved Ding Dongs and Spaghettio's. Today's organic-food-eating children have no idea the greatness that could be found in boxes and cans of preservatives and sugar, though I am guessing these things are no longer tops on your list of favorites. Your taste buds changed, yet you did not judge them for changing or insist that they remain the same. I'm not still chowing down on chocolate hockey pucks that never expire while I watch the Flintstones because "by golly, that was my favorite thing in 1986!" So why does our taste for life have to remain the same as the day we chose a college major or accepted a position? Maybe you were only meant to camp there. A temporary dwelling. It was not intended to be the last job you ever take.

One of the best depictions of this that I have ever heard came from the movie Fight Club. As Edward Norton watches his house burn down, he says, "It's just, when you buy furniture, you tell yourself, that's it. That's the last sofa I'm going to need. Whatever else happens, I've got that sofa problem handled." Then something happens, and we no longer have the sofa problem solved. We have to start all over. No one wants to be without a couch. It makes the house feel empty, just as being without a career or best friend or mate can make life feel meaningless.

When I first got divorced, I had to buy a new couch. I cannot tell you how frustrating it is to buy something that you already own, so I wanted to get it over with. For most of us lucky first world country-dwellers, a couch isn't a luxury, and it is a necessity. I spent months shopping for a couch and then made the last minute, horrible decision that I regretted until I finally was able to get rid of it. I am sure you can relate. Perhaps you have your own ugly couch that you are dying to get rid of, be it a relationship, job, or position on the PTA that you knew you didn't have time to do. We all have those boxes we want to be checked, which makes us too quick to buy something that is not meant for us and is not even what we really desire.

While roots are significant, we need to be free from our incessant need for external stability. Oftentimes, it is in the fluidity of change that we grow the most. After leaving that job, I went into business for myself. It was scary! But I can honestly say that it was not as frightening as I had always assumed it would be. For the first year, I woke up thankful, and a little shocked, every time I paid my mortgage. Though I am still grateful, now it has now become a natural way of life. I honestly cannot imagine going back to working for someone else. I set my own hours. I work less in the summers so that I can spend afternoons kayaking with my son. I have paid off the debt that previously felt like an impossibility. And this is all just the beginning. I have only been doing this for two years; who knows what things will look like in ten years?!

I see the woman in that picture, and I want to hug her excitedly and tell her she has no idea the fantastic ride on which she is about to embark. She had better unpack those boxes quickly because she will need to be mobile and able to move fast. Her life is about to take off. And so is yours. Take a moment and imagine your own "burning house" moment. What baggage do you need to unpack to be ready for the next step?

Let's start with the classic fear of failure. It can be absolutely paralyzing. Break it down. As we discussed earlier, it is important to specifically define our goals, fears, and judgments to deal with them appropriately. Ask yourself what a failure for you is? Is it not being successful? Is it only being mediocre? Having others mock you? How do YOU define failure? My guess is that it is pretty ambiguous. And it is difficult to refute an ill-defined fear. Figure out precisely what it is that you fear.

Assume your fear becomes a reality. What is the worst that can happen? For me, I decided the worst outcome would be that I would be unable to pay my bills. I have been poor before. Don't get me started on my sad tales of working three jobs in college and not having fifty cents to vacuum my car at the car wash. I lived on the 3rd floor of my apartment complex and would string five extension cords together to vacuum my car in the parking lot. While the idea of going back to those days was not particularly thrilling for me, I knew I was able to make money if I needed to. I decided I could always be an Uber driver. There was no way that I would lose my house. I had a backup plan. (As a side note, I am an admittedly horrible driver, so I am almost sure that God blessed my efforts as a gift to humanity to NOT have me drive for Uber. He says, "you're welcome, world.")

If you were to go back to school or switch jobs or start a new career, what is the worst that can happen? Make a list. What if you don't get the job? You don't have it now. Maybe you don't pass the class you need to take. Not passing means you don't get credit for it. I don't know how else to tell you this, but you aren't getting credit now. You are therefore already experiencing the exact same consequences you fear most.

"But," you say," what if I'm not good at it?" Now we have probably hit on the real essence of the fear. Not being good enough. What is good? Do you have to be the best in your field? In your office? According to who's standard? Let me tell you that unless you are an Olympic athlete, there is probably not a way to measure who is the "best" at much of anything.

One of my best friends, who is also a psychologist, texted me about her day. She had a rough day because one of her colleagues had gotten Christmas gifts from many of her clients and she had not. Not that my friend cared about the gifts, but this tangible discrepancy made her question her own effectiveness. Here's the truth: My friend is a brilliant psychologist. She works with male veterans who have PTSD and substance use issues. They are probably not gift givers to ANYONE. It's an incredibly difficult population because most of these men are in a really (really!) bad place. Success for her clients is actually going to their appointment on any given day. So how do you measure how successful she is? Is it contingent upon her clients' full recovery? If they show up? Days of sobriety? Or that she is keeping them alive? Giving them hope? What IS enough to be enough? It is an act of cruelty to judge yourself against a standard that is impossible to define, therefore completely impossible to ever meet.

Stop being cruel to yourself. Ask yourself, what is it that defines success for you? How will you know when you are "there?" What do you consider failure? And I suggest you make it a reasonable standard. Basing it on accolades or financial rewards is probably not the best gauge. I had some amazing teachers growing up who's name you will never know. It does not lessen their ability or make them a failure.

———◆———

When considering a big leap, do a cost-benefit analysis. In my situation with my previous job, I had a flexible schedule that allowed me to work later some days so that I could leave by 3 p.m. several days per week to pick up my son. He has always come first, and that was not going to change. I was well aware that no other full-time job would grant me such flexibility. Therefore, I didn't have a choice —I knew I had to create my own position in order to continue to prioritize my son in the way that I wanted to. The potential costs, both figurative and literal, did not compare to the benefits offered by a 4' tall redhead who makes my heart smile.

What are the potential costs to the leap you are eyeing? Write them down. Be realistic. And then be realistic about the potential benefits. After all, what if you DON'T fail? What if it works? Someone invented the pool noodle and is a millionaire, y' all. You never know what could change your life in a significant way. Give yourself some credit.

Starting from the outside in, rather than the inside out, is another big box in the trunk that keeps us from following our dreams. We look to others to define our dreams for us. We don't know who we are, so we allow other people to define us. "You aren't made for that. You should stick with what you know." We listen as other people speak to what they perceive are our abilities instead of what our gut screams. We end up acting out the script of what should maybe be someone else's life. Unfortunately, that script inevitably includes their own fears, as well.

Someone who fears heights will not tell you to take a leap. Having a son who is part monkey made me painfully aware of this natural tendency to pass on our fears to others. I always like to clarify that I am not afraid of heights; I am so scared of falling from them. Deathly afraid. Climbing heights without walls or bars to hold onto is therefore terrifying to me. From the first day, he came to our home as a 4-year-old, he was hanging upside down from the outside of the nets on the play equipment that were meant to keep kids safely inside. Internally, I wanted to grab him and tell him to come down immediately, but I knew that would be doing him a disservice. I would be instilling in him MY fear of heights. The truth is, the kid is a crazy good climber. He has "sticky feet" that seem to grab onto anything. He has brute upper arm strength to hold on and a razor-sharp focus that keeps him from seeing a squirrel and tumbling down. So I let him do it. I watched, thinking of the worst possible outcome, most likely a broken arm. I decided I could handle a broken arm far easier than him living a lifetime being afraid of something he is naturally good at simply because his mother was worried. Don't inherit someone else's fears. Climb outside of the net and decide for yourself how scary it is. You might find your own brute strength can carry you much further than you ever thought possible.

It's also time to unload the box of approval-seeking. Do you need others to sign off on your decisions? Maybe you are still seeking the approval of your parents. Or a hard-to-please spouse. Or the hardest to please of all, that imaginary audience in your own head. Psychologist Erick Erickson developed a concept he called the "imaginary audience." Essentially, most of us walk around, assuming that others are watching – and judging – our every move. They notice the spot of mustard on our shirt. They see us when we trip over curbs. They chat in the break room about the typo we made in our last email. It's as if we all think we live on the Truman Show, our every move under the microscope of scrutiny of those around us.

Here's a first-world problem for you. When I was

in high school, I decided I should tag my clothes with the day I wore them so I would not repeat them too soon. Because why? The other kids had some hidden calendar tracking my wardrobe? My 36-year-old self sees so many layers of ridiculousness in this whole concept; I don't even feel the need to expand upon them. My 16-year-old self was genuinely concerned. That poor girl so desperately wanted to fit in, be liked, and to be "cool," whatever the heck that is. I wish I could go back and hug her and tell her in the most loving way possible to get over herself. I want to share with her this secret: No one could possibly track my clothes because they were all too busy trying to hide their own mustard stains and not trip over the curbs along their own path.

Let me tell you the same secret: No one is watching. And if they do have time to watch what you are doing that closely, then they are obviously not focused on the heights they are climbing themselves, and they could fall at any moment. Do people judge others? Yes. For sure. Indubitably (I love that word!). You have to ask yourself, who do you want in your studio audience? If your life is a reality show, then to whom would you give tickets? Would you give them to the snarky girl in the next office over? Or would you give them to the friend who baked you cookies on your last birthday? You get to choose who gets a say in your life. Tickets are not handed out by default to your mother because she birthed you. It is your choice. You can love her without giving her a say in your life today. You can be selective about everyone else who has a ticket to your life, your ideas, and your thoughts.

There is a verse in the Bible that warns against "throwing your pearls to the swine." Now I am not calling your Aunt Cathy a pig, but…if someone snorts and throws mud all over your ideas and accomplishments, then the warning applies. Be careful who you share your dreams and ideas with before they are ready to be birthed. The most fragile time in the development of any living thing is infancy. Hence most new moms arm themselves with hand sanitizer like they are starting an anti-germ militia. Cough around a newborn and see how quickly you get exiled from baby snuggles. You must learn to protect your dreams and progress with the same tenacity. Even well-meaning people can spew questions and disapproval, destroying them before they have a chance to develop.

Learn to shut out negativity. Negativity and constructive criticism are not the same things. Constructive means "serving a useful purpose; tending to build up." It helps you grow. I have a friend, Korby, reading this book for me as I write. If all she handed me back were hearts and stars telling me how great it is, that would not be helpful. I need her to be real. I need her to give me honest feedback because that's how I grow. That isn't negativity. It is constructive. As you fill your audience, I pray you to give tickets to the Korbys of your life who will tell you that you use the word "so" too much. You should also give them to the cheerleaders who encourage you to keep going, and to the faithful cookie bakers who keep you fueled for the journey. Most of all, I pray you to give your tickets deliberately and with discernment, not by default.

Unfortunately, many people have had more than just a mere nay-sayer in their audience. Some of you have been abused – physically, emotionally, or sexually. You have had people demean you and make you feel worthless. You carry those voices with you in your head today. You are allowing someone who never deserved a second of your time to continue to influence your life decades later. Ask yourself who first told you that you were a failure or had nothing to offer other than your body. It is time to clean out your audience. Kick out the voice of your abuser. They no longer get space in your life. What and who you listen to is YOUR choice now. You are in charge of your own ticket distribution. Don't waste them.

Another major box to unload is the fear of the unknown. It is easy to get bogged down in the need to know how the story ends before you begin it. An African Gazelle can jump 10 feet in the air and cover a distance of 30 feet; however, they are kept in fences that are only 3 feet high in zoos around the country because they won't jump where they can't see. They have no idea how strong and powerful they really are. One little leap, and they would find freedom without fences. And so could you. How often are we confined by the limitations of our own vision?

Psalm 119:105 says, "Your word is a lamp unto my

feet and a light unto my path." I don't know about y' all, but I wish it were a street lamp unto my feet and a stadium light unto my path. Lights along a pathway don't always offer much light, which can be unnerving. I went hiking at night once. I have never been so scared while hiking in my life. I had a tiny lamp in my hand and had to focus on my every step because I could not see what was ahead of me on the trail. What I didn't realize is that I didn't need to. As long as I could see my next step, I was safe. No cliff was going to jump out and send me hurling below. No giant rock was going to fall from the sky and make me trip. Those were unrealistic fears based on my own need to know. All I needed to see to be safe was the next step. And the next step. And the next, until I made it to the top. That is all you need, too, my friend. Just keep your mind focused on the next step.

It's time to start moving a little faster. Find a new route. Take the next step you need to make that major life change. The worst that can happen is your shoes get a little dirty.

"Faith is taking the first step even when you don't see the whole staircase."
~ Marin Luther King, Jr

CHAPTER 8: SAVE YOUR OWN DANG SEAT

REMEMBER THAT AWKWARD MOMENT OF walking in the lunchroom as a kid and trying to find a seat? The rejection potential of that situation was off the charts. It's like looking for the least disgusting toilet in an airport bathroom. After a while, you realize they're all next to something potentially crappy. Occasionally, a wonderful soul would wave me over, having saved me a seat next to them, thus eliminating the frantic scanning and deliberation. In actuality, it was just a place to park your hiney for 20 minutes while you stuffed your face, though 12-year-old me felt it was a monumental decision with grave ramifications on my self-esteem. I always wanted someone who would "save me a seat" in life. I wanted someone who would make sure I had a place to fit in and feel at home. I would do the same for them. We all crave a place where we feel like we fit in and belong.

There's a concept in child development called the "secure base." Watch any group of 3-4-year-olds. They will run away from their parent to play, running back periodically to make sure that mom has not left, will still accept them, and most likely to make sure she is still offering goldfish crackers. This process of leaving and coming back teaches them that it is okay to leave the security of home because it will always be there when they come back. Who doesn't want that no matter how old you are?! (And let's be real, those cheesy little fish crackers are addictive.) Though I am a raging extravert, I don't like going to events alone. I prefer to walk in with someone next to me. Then, we can talk to each other if no one else wants to talk to us. If I want to explore, there is someone by my side to get lost in the hallways with me, which I always seem to do. If there is a way to end up in the kitchen, storage closet, or back alley entrance, I will find it. It is my superpower.

Unfortunately, many of us have never had that person to save us a seat. Maybe you don't have a safe place to retreat when the world begins to close in on you. In that case, you have to create that safe space for yourself. Some people are born with a safety net. Others have to weave their own. Be it financially, emotionally, relationally; somewhere along the way you are going to have to find some string and get to work. I googled "how to make a net" and found these three tools are all you need to get started: a foundation, string, and a mesh stick. Y'all get ready because this will preach.

Let's start with the foundation. This is the most important part because it is what you will build everything else on. If it is weak, then the whole net will collapse and ain't nobody got time for that. Your foundation is the place of absolute truth.

What you KNOW to be true. What truth have you learned about yourself absolutely over the years? Is it that you are a survivor? That you are resilient and find a way to bounce back? Are those things never truly as bad as they seem? When I was in 7th grade, I had a huge crush on Randy Hair. One day, my dear friend Meredith decided to tell him I had a crush on him. Given that I had zero game at the time, this pretty much meant I could never show my face at school again. I remember journaling pages about this great tragedy and its mortal consequences as I bawled my eyes out. Reading over those pages a few years later, I smiled at how something could be such a big deal at the moment, yet not matter in the long run. Your crisis may be far more serious than the "Great Randy Hair Reveal" tragedy, but the principle remains the same. Time truly does heal almost all wounds. Or at least make them more bearable. Over time, we gain more resources to cope, find greater truths, and hopefully, stumble upon a measure of grace from which we can find relief from the judgments in our own minds. Perspective can be a beautiful thing.

If you are still struggling to make your foundation, try changing your perspective. Put your life story in the center of the room. Now imagine yourself taking about ten steps back and turning to the left about 45 degrees. Try to see it from outside of yourself. Give yourself credit you would give someone else. Allow yourself to see the progress you've made, the strength you have shown, and the ways you could have fallen apart but instead somehow came together. Take some time and write down your story. Tell it to yourself, start to finish. You will find that you have faired far better than you thought. When you add up the sum total of your tears and years, it is probably far more than you realized as you were living it. There are a million places where you could have broken but didn't. You are still here. Use that to find your truth. And for the love of all that is good and holy, give yourself a break. Enough already.

Let's assume you have found your truth, any truth, to serve as your foundation. That's all you need to begin to build. Now you need some string. This is where it gets fun. Strings can be anything. Anything that is a piece of your authentic self. Issues most often tend to arise when we are not true to our values. Values are "one's definition of what's important in life." They are the glue that holds us together, or in this case, the strings that build our net. What makes you, you? Is it your love of learning? Your affection for the great outdoors? Your spontaneous spirit? Maybe you value challenge, growth, authenticity, or adventure. Values are like colors. None are better than the others. All serve a purpose. Even brown, which I hate, makes a nice pair of boots, whereas pink is lovely for cupcake frosting but does not look so great on me. Not every color is for everyone in every situation. Values are the same way. None are bad, but some define you better than others.

Learning, recreation, health, and relationships are all categories of values. Most people need a good balance of all these types. When life gets busy, we tend to take out the "extras" first that are usually most important to us to give us time and resources to do all the things we "have" to do. While this may sound like the grown-up, the responsible thing to do, it can easily leave us feeling empty and missing part of ourselves.

Take some time to write down the things that are most important to you. Take out the "shoulds" of what should be important and focus on what matters to you most. Pause and ask yourself where your values came from. Is it something you were taught is important? Or something that is important to you. For example, I am not a detail-oriented person. I am all forest and no trees when it comes to vision. For years, I would say that it was my goal to be more detail-oriented, but I never met that goal. Shoot, I didn't even know how to start. To be honest, I LIKE being a big-picture person. It is an asset for me that has served me well. Changing that was a giant "should" because it was something I had been told that I should do by others, well-meaning or not, and not an actual value of mine. This meant I was repeatedly shaming myself for missing the mark on something I never cared enough to put effort to. As I changed this perspective, I noticed that the people who tended to tell me all of the little things that I should do in order to be successful are still sitting on the sidelines making plans while I am already in the game executing them. It is far past time to ditch the shoulds and find your own values.

There are some great values inventories online

that you can take to help you define what's most important to you. Once you have a grasp on your values, take a moment to evaluate how close or far you are from fleshing out those values in your day-to-day life. Take a close look at your net. Maybe the pattern isn't developing as you want it to. That's okay. Just take a step back and figure out the direction in which you want your thread to go and start weaving. Slowly but surely, you will build your net the way YOU want it to look.

Once you have found the strings with which you will weave your net, you need a mesh stick. Why, you ask? What the heck is a mesh stick, you ask? It's a shuttle or the piece you will use to push the string in and out to weave the net. It's your motivation. What will keep you going on days that are hard? What will propel you from one section of your day to another?

I had a side hustle for a while with a remarkable skin care company (seriously, the first few years after my divorce should have aged me like a president. Here is a shout out to having good eye cream!). In all the pieces of training, we were taught that you start with your "why." Your "why" is your motivation for doing this business. And, "your why should make you cry." You see, when you own your own business, there is no one demanding that you put in hours, making sure you follow up with leads, etc. It's all on you. So you had better have something to make you want to do it. If it's not powerful enough to make you tear up when you think about what it means to you, then it probably won't be enough to motivate you to turn off Netflix and get on the phone, where you will likely be rejected a decent portion of the time.

We all need to find our "why." I believe that is true for anything we do in life that requires a lot of energy. Change is hard. And usually long. I need a darn good mesh stick to keep pushing me through if I am going to get it done and not just settle for the status quo. Think about what keeps you going. Maybe it's your kids (which seems like the cop-out mom answer, but is usually true), or the hope of children in the future. Perhaps it's your dreams you had as a child that have been deferred but not forgotten. Whatever it is, you wouldn't be reading this book if something deep inside of you didn't believe that there was more. More healing. More joy. More purpose. More of this life left to take in. Find that belief and let it be your mesh stick, your "why," your driving force. And start weaving that net!

Once you have your net woven, something amazing happens. You can make your own seat. I'm not negating the importance of having someone save you a seat. There's something heartwarming about that. But if you find yourself tired of standing around, waiting on someone else to make room so you can finally sit, it is nice to have one handy. It takes so much of the pressure off frantically trying to find a place to fit in in a crowded room. And, it is very difficult to feel like I have a purpose when I don't even have a place to rest my bum. Once you find your seat, you are now free to settle in and figure out why you are there and what you want to do with your time in that room. The choice is ALL yours.

I love being a "plus one" at events because I love getting dressed up, and my FOMO is legit. But something happens that I don't love so much when I am at someone else's table. I suddenly lose my ability to make decisions about when to arrive, eat, leave, etc.… I tend to defer to the host out of a sense of social politeness. It's their table. Their seat that you are in. They make decisions on how the evening goes. However, when I buy my own ticket, I come and go as I please and make my own decisions. It is much the same way with finding your way in life. Weave your own seat. Know your value and absolve yourself from all "shoulds." This will free you to use your seat; however, you please as a base from which to do all of the things you were meant to do.

There is also a great paradox in life that reigns true: As you learn to be comfortable on your own, you will find you are more comfortable with others.

Maybe it's something about having your own chair that makes people feel as if you might have room for them to sit, too. Or at least they feel comfortable that you won't steal their own hard-earned spot.

———◆———

I am learning, slowly, that finding yourself in another person is a dangerous thing. Real love is not very romantic. The famous scene in Jerry McGuire, where Tom Cruise professes his love and says, "you complete me" sounds wonderful in a sound byte but think about it. When two healthy people enter into a relationship, both should already be complete. Can you imagine going on a date with someone who had a gaping hole in their side? And yet, that's how so many of us walk around. We are unsure of ourselves, waiting for someone else to fill our gaps like a can of fix-a-flat.

I worked with troubled teenagers for many years. Most of these kids had abusive parents, non-existent fathers, and minimal resources. I saw 16-year-old girls who were TRYING to get pregnant. Over and over, they would say they that they just wanted someone to love and to love them back. We all have a need to be loved, and most of us will fill it any way we can, be it with food, sex, alcohol, or even kids. Since we were made with this need, it's nothing to be ashamed of. Our Creator gets it, and I truly believe that God will send you people to fill in the gaps of those that are missing. When we are walking around waiting for someone to fill in the gaps of OURSELVES, we will inevitably end up creating a more disastrous situation for everyone. Two broken people don't make a whole. They simply make a bigger hole.

You have to know who you are before you can introduce yourself to someone else. In the movie, Runaway Bride, it is pointed out that Julia Roberts character always orders the same type of eggs as the man she is dating. There's an awesome scene in which she makes all the different types of eggs, and tries them all, and concludes that she does not even like eggs. What about you? What kind of eggs do you like? What music makes you want to dance? Do you even like to dance? These may seem like trivial aspects of who you are, but nothing about you is trivial. It is one thing to choose to eat Indian food that you hate on occasion because your partner loves it, but it's another to feel as if you must eat it in order to be accepted by them. But worse still: to not even know if you actually like Indian food.

Take a few minutes and make a list of things about you. Write down the things that make your heart smile and things that make you want to cry. Identify pivotal moments in your life that are now a part of your story. Write down what you learned from them about who you are and what you want in this life. Then, make a list of things that scare you. There's a coaching directive which states you should do one thing that scares you every day. It is only in reaching our limits that we learn to go beyond them. In the famous words of Winnie the

Pooh, "Promise me you'll always remember: You're braver than you believe and stronger than you seem, and smarter than you think." Get the tattoo. Go skydiving. Register for the 5k. Take a dance lesson. Book the trip. Try curry. Karaoke. Paint your front door. Even if it doesn't work out, you will gain more information about who you are and, just as importantly, who you aren't.

Find your values. Define your "why" and let it push you a little more each day. Keep weaving that seat. When you finish your chair, you can share helpful weaving tips with someone else as they begin to weave their own. And it will be beautiful because you will have plenty of string, lots of motivation and enough experience to make it one that will last.

"The only person you are destined to become is the person you decide to be."
~ Ralph Waldo Emerson

CHAPTER 9: CHANGE THE WORLD

LEONARD DAVINCI SAID, "TIME STAYS long enough for anyone who will use it." And use it, he did. In the 1400s DaVinci invented the first parachute, sketching out a design on which modern parachutes are based. The irony of this is that airplanes, which would create a need for parachutes, would not be invented for another 400 years. Though I am sure DaVinci did not have a tangible purpose in mind for all that the parachute could do, he still believed it was needed. Today, the parachute has been used in multiple capacities, from soldiers in warfare, to first world thrill-seekers crossing off a bucket list item, and (most importantly) parachute day in P.E. class. There was nothing like running under that thing while it floated above you. Though he never knew that his design of the parachute worked, Leonardo DiVinci changed the world with a simple sketch.

Most of us would love to change the world. While that sounds catchy and inspiring, maybe the world doesn't need us to change it. Not to say that there aren't some horrible things that happen on a daily basis. I was reading headlines about children killing children, corrupt world leaders, and other unspeakable crimes around the world. There are certainly some things that need to go. And, quite frankly, some people. But if you are struggling with where to start, what if, just for today, you focused on accepting the world as it is instead of changing it? Could that ironically be the first step in making it a better place?

There's a concept in Dialectical Behavior Therapy (DBT) called radical acceptance. Radical acceptance is basically the idea that sometimes we have to take life on life's terms. The old "it is what it is" concept. No one likes that idea. If something in my life does not look the way I want it to, my first response is not to shake my head and say, "Oh, well. That's just how it is." In fact, I am the extreme opposite of that. I am a believer in the impossible, the ultimate eternal optimist. I once bought these adorable gold sandals. I even splurged and got the $40 sandals instead of the $20 ones because these were so perfect. A few days later, I went on a trip and (I think) left one in the hotel. However, it went down, I came home with just one shoe. That shoe lived in my closet for the next two years in hopes of the other one appearing one day to live with its "sole mate." (Oh, come on…you know that was a good one). The day I threw that lonely right shoe away, I was still convinced that the other one would probably appear the next day as a lesson that I should have never given up.

Here's the deal: Sometimes the shoe is just lost. The marriage is over. The money is gone. The friendship has ended. The Titanic is sunk. Some stories are not going to end any differently, no matter how much we keep hoping that they will. This leaves you with a choice. You can keep waiting for change, which inevitably leads to suffering as you long for things to be different. Or you can get rid of the painful reminders of what was lost, throw away the dang shoe, suck it up and buy a new pair. Guess what?! You are worth not just one pair of the $40 shoes, but TWO because life is too short to pine away for one gold shoe when there are so many others left in the store.

When we choose to accept a situation as it is radically, we will likely feel a surge of pain. This is normal as we grieve the loss of our ideals. I got married at the ripe old age of 22. My husband was in the Air Force and was "specially selected" for an internship in Biloxi, Mississippi. That's a military euphemism for "ordered." This meant leaving all my friends and family and postponing graduate school, all while adjusting to life as a military wife. We had been there for less than a week when it hit me: I was stuck. I had my first panic attack ever as I ugly cried for hours. My poor young groom listened as I repeatedly screamed, "It doesn't matter! It doesn't matter if I love it here or hate it. I CAN'T LEAVE! We are trapped!!" I felt as if my world were closing in on me. I had never been in a situation where I felt so powerless before. I am not about to tell you that after that moment of dramatic realization that I fell in love with Biloxi and birds began to sing around my head while I frolicked in the sand. The sand would have definitely been the only place I frolicked on that beach anyways. I was dang sure I wouldn't be getting in that brown water. I can tell you that I radically accepted that I was there. I clearly couldn't go anywhere else, so I started looking for a job, found a church, began volunteering on base, and asked anyone I could find to grab a coffee and be my new friend. I even swam in the ocean. You see, I had to accept my situation before I could deal with it effectively. Had I continued to spend my time wishing I was somewhere else, I would have continued to suffer the loss of those things over and over. Every day would have brought more of the same grief, like the movie Groundhog Day, but with more tears and less Bill Murray. And let's be real, I don't care what color the water is, a beach is a beach. You might as well jump in and embrace it.

What are you refusing to accept? What are you pining away for? What do you aimlessly wish would change? What if instead of waiting on the world to change, you chose to accept it just as it is? What if you got up today and did the things that you need to do to make today better, even in its crappy current state?

Radical acceptance can feel like we are giving up hope. So here is a question: Is hope a bad thing or a good thing? In Shawshank Redemption, Tim Robbins' character Andy says, "Hope is a good thing, maybe the best of things. And no good thing ever dies." To which Red, played by the great Morgan Freeman, replies, "Hope is a dangerous thing. It can drive a man insane." Both are true. Hope is perhaps the most powerful two-edged sword in human existence. It can both keep you going and keep you stuck in a place you are not meant to be. Thus, it takes a careful stance to balance between accepting reality and striving for change.

I believe you can have both. My entire profession is based on the idea that people can learn, change, and grow no matter what has happened to them. Add faith in an all-powerful God, and I basically believe that Michael Jackson could rise from the dead and ride in on a unicorn to hand me a million dollars at any given moment. No matter the situation, I always have hope that it can - and will- be better. Still, I cannot base my happiness, healing, or any other decisions on this hope. Those must be based purely on the reality of the situation in its current state.

The distinction between relying on hope and having hope can be a difficult, yet critical, one to understand. Having hope keeps me going. When things look bleak, hope tells me that they won't always be this way. I have to keep pressing forward. Relying on hope, on the other hand, prevents me from pressing forward because I have a magical belief that things will just BE better. This is dangerous because it not only ignores logic but also discounts my role in the course of events. There's an old saying that one must "pray like it depends on God and work as it depends on you." That is the case with hope. Hope as if anything is possible, but work as if you have to make it happen. And most importantly, you must remember that no amount of hope, faith, or unicorn dust can change someone who does not want to change.

A common question that arises in therapy is, "should I talk to (insert difficult person) about (insert difficult topic)?" The answer is, it depends on what your goal is. If your goal is to get an apology, understanding, or even acknowledgment, it is probably a bad idea. We cannot guarantee how another person will respond. However, if having the conversation will give you a sense of peace, resolution, or a sense of accomplishment for using your voice, then, by all means, you should do it. The decision to do anything that relies on another person should never be based on the outcome. That is far beyond our control. It's okay to hope it will go well but to make a decision based on such hope would be foolish.

We must learn to deal with life on life's terms, rather than our own. Let me say for the record that if I had my way, the terms would be much more efficient. I have had many experiences in my life that involved a lot of waiting. These stories end gloriously and are some of my most precious testimonies, but the waiting was not so glorious. It involved many nights of crying on my floor and begging God to move NOW. Quite frankly, I am thankful that I had stained concrete in my living room because wood floors would have certainly warped under my tears. I cannot explain the timing. But I do know this: There is so much growth that happens in times of waiting.

Waiting allows time for our superfluous outer layers

to fall off. Scientists in China examined the outer shell of a lotus seed using carbon dating technology. They discovered this particular seed was over 2,000 years old. Now, I sincerely hope you do not find yourself waiting 2,000 years to blossom into whatever life has for you. Still, you gotta hand it to that seed for having some crazy perseverance. In order to germinate, which that very old seed did, the lotus seed requires the perfect combination of sun, water, and muddy soil to break its hard, outer shell and grow into the beautiful flower it is. Who knows why this poor seed didn't find that combo in all that time? Yet, it remained intact until it was finally able to fulfill its purpose of producing beautiful flowers. Though your wait may be long, you must keep your vision and your resources intact until the timing is right for your purpose to be fulfilled.

An interesting note about the Lotus: once grown, the Lotus sinks back into the mud at night, only to bloom again clean the next day. The great Chinese Philosopher Confucius wrote, "I have a love for the Lotus while growing in mud it still remains unstained." I believe waiting does many things for us. It prepares us to blossom in muddy situations without being stained by the world around us. It creates in us an inoculation against the things that would dull our shine if they were handed to us. It softens the hardest parts of our shell so that nutrients can get in and the potential of the seed can be released. None of us this makes me enjoy waiting anymore, but it does allow me to look back and see that time spent waiting allowed me to learn and grow far more than any other type of season in my life. And it solidifies that the world does not turn on my clock but on something far bigger and greater than myself. While humbling, that is generally a message that often needs repeating.

In my clinical practice, I see a constant search for control. People make up some pretty elaborate rules in order to give structure to life, which is not meant to be so strictly structured. I call these structures toothpick houses. These rules give us a false sense of safety as they make us believe that if we do x, y and z, we can avoid the horrible outcome we fear. Or we can make sense of something that is nonsensical. They are toothpick houses because one tiny burst of air or bump of the table, and they all fall down; they don't protect us from anything. In fact, they can be dangerous. I once knew of a man that died from swallowing a toothpick. He had a habit of sucking on them and accidentally swallowed one while being robbed. He was so focused on the robbery that he thought nothing of it, yet It punctured his innards, causing internal damage. So many times, we focus on the thing that happens TO us and forget about what is happening IN us, which can be far more menacing in the long run.

The problem with control Is that it's little more than a dangerous illusion. For example, I may believe that if I keep myself guarded, not opening up to others or letting them in, I will not get hurt. This makes me feel in control of my emotions and the outcome of any relationship. When I decide that I do want to build a relationship, I don't know-how. My emotions won't let me open up. I am no longer free to engage with others as I want. I avoid events where a connection is a possibility. I withdraw from my family and stop answering my phone. What I thought I was controlling is controlling me. Having control means I am free to turn something off and on whenever I want. The second I am not free to turn off my "alarms" when I want, then I have lost control. We don't have control. We have choices.

Stephen Covey said, "We see the world not as it is but as we are." Today, you have a choice. You can choose to see your world, not as a collection of broken pieces that require fixing, but as a mosaic of individual experiences that each has meaning and purpose all their own. I cannot begin to arrange pieces until I accept the size and shape and position of each one as it is. Otherwise, I will spend all my time wishing that the round piece in front of me had a few more corners so it could serve as an edge piece. And that, my friends, is not only futile; it is the definition of insanity. Once I take stock of where I have been and accurately assess my current position in life, then I can make an educated decision about where to go from here. It all begins with a big helping of acceptance a side of giving up the idea of control.

When I stop trying to change things, I realize how beautifully the world is able to shift all on its own. It doesn't have to change for me to find peace. There is a tremendous peace that comes with simply being present in this moment just as it is.

"As I get older, the more I stay focused on the acceptance of myself and others and choose compassion over judgment and curiosity over fear."
~ Tracee Ellis Ross

CHAPTER 10: FIND YO'SELF

I GREW UP IN A RELATIVELY small town. The closest shopping mall was almost two hours away. Twice a year, for school clothes and Christmas shopping, we planned trips to the mall. It was an all-day affair. We would spend hours at the mall, followed by a trip to Target to get essentials, with dinner at Applebee's thrown in because we didn't have that in my town, either. I remember thinking as a kid, "I wonder what it would be like to live in a town with a mall. I would be so broke because I would go there every day and shop." I don't know if my ten-year-old self would be disappointed or proud that I live in a town with five malls and haven't been to a single one of them in months.

So often we think we know what we want or what would make us happy, but we really have no clue. Many times, just as my childhood self wondered about my ability to abstain from shopping, we also lack trust in our own ability to forego things that are not in our best interest. We have a concept of ourselves based on limited experiences and internalized judgments. This distrust causes us to find "solutions" to protect us from ourselves. My shopping judgments were just one indicator of my lack of confidence in my choices.

On a much more serious note, I suffered from an eating disorder for years as a teenager and young adult. While there is no silver bullet answer to explain why someone develops an eating disorder, there are certain standard features that can be found. Like many others who suffer, my extreme distrust of myself led me to set up countless food rules by which to live. In my mind, without these rules, I would have just spent my whole life devouring one large pizza after another, stopping only to add a few cartons of ice cream in between.

This distrust carried over into every decision that I made. I continously questioned my own judgment. Did I pick the right college? The right mate? Did I spend too much money? Did I buy the right thing? It was a line of questioning and second-guessing in my head. Y'all, before the days of smartphones with calculators, I would stand in the store solving complex algebra equations to figure out what the best deal was on EVERYTHING. Toilet paper math is a special kind of hard. Double rolls, triple rolls, 147 rolls free... what does one even do with all that? There is no way I could pass that test, so I was always left feeling like I missed the mark.

Ultimately, my indecision had nothing to do with food, shopping malls, toilet paper, or anything else. It was all rooted in my own self-doubt and lack of trust in my ability to make good decisions independently. To move beyond this, and for Pete's sake, to move through the toilet paper aisle a little faster, I had to learn that I was someone worth trusting. I might be a hot mess, and I assure you I don't always get it right, but I am still fully capable of making decisions for myself. And so are you. You may not believe it now, so you have to demonstrate this to yourself. Practice in small ways. Choose the restaurant when you go out. Pick the movie. Just make a decision and run with it. Even if it sucks, you will have learned a little more about what you like and don't like. A little more about YOU: and you, my friend, are so worth learning about!

My biggest hope for you is that you take time to get to know your authentic self —the you that exists apart from who anyone says you are and who you feel should be. Learn about what makes you smile and what makes you cry. Find the rhythm of your own body. Maybe you function best waking up at sunrise and going to bed early. Perhaps you're a night owl. Maybe you prefer a big breakfast to a big dinner. Imagine you are the proud owner of a brand new super machine that can take you on adventures, help you succeed in your job, make you a better partner and open doors to a more enjoyable life. Wouldn't you read the manual cover to cover, memorizing every detail? Learning what it runs on, how to reach optimal performance, and what pitfalls to avoid that could break it? Come close and let me tell you a secret: You not only have that machine; you are that machine! Your body is a vehicle that can do amazing things for you. It is your job to figure out how it runs best and give it a kickstart.

How often do we allow others to define our

strengths and weaknesses rather than following our own sense of self? Maybe you have heard the words, "people in our family can't do that…" Or, "you just aren't made for that." Why does someone else get to say what you can or cannot do? I am not saying everyone can do everything. I'm 5'9. I will never be a jockey, even though I do love a good horse race. What I am saying is that it is up to you to figure out what your own mind, body, and soul can do.

I have wanted to be a psychologist since I was eight years old. I have also always wanted to adopt children. At age 30, I had just gotten licensed as a psychologist. My precious son, for whom I had prayed for so long, was placed with us that year, too. I was married. We had a charming home. I remember laying by the kiddie pool while my son played, the sun beating down on me and a Kenny Chesney song playing in the background. I lay there at that moment, thinking I finally had everything I ever wanted. I still smile when I hear that song, thinking of that incredible feeling of such pure contentment.

One year later, I was living in a small apartment, sharing custody of my son during my pending divorce. Even the kiddie pool was gone. Other than the bathrobe I have had since 2001, very little else has stayed the same in my life over the last five years. I have lost relationships, money, a job that I loved, and so much more. Some of the change is a product of my own choices, good and bad. Some is a product of life. All of it combined is my story. It is all that led me to this place at this moment. In the middle of all that loss, I gained me. I found out that I am genuinely braver than I thought and stronger than I could have ever imagined. I also found life-long friendships and more support and love that I ever knew existed. Only in having everything stripped away, did I learn what belonged in my life and how to be comfortable in my own skin.

Before my life was mostly leveled flat, I did not know who I was. I was much like Julia Roberts in Runaway Bride with the eggs. I used to like the same type of music as whoever I was dating. I am pretty easy-going, so I often picked up the same hobbies as my significant other because I can have fun doing almost anything. I had no clue what I truly enjoyed and what my preferences were.

My then-husband and I used to frequently hike and camp. We had a goal to hike the highest point of every state. We completed 28 of the 50. I know…it sounds cool. I have since realized that while I like hiking okay, I don't like camping at all. It smells funny and is a lot of work. I would rather go to a hotel at the end of the day to shower and watch HGTV. These are things I discovered as I allowed myself the freedom to make my own choices, whatever they might be. Take time to get to know yourself. Take yourself to dinner. Try a new hobby. You might find new talent. Or discover that you don't like to get dirty. Either way, I pray you to stumble upon something you truly love in the pro-cess, and most of all someone you truly love — the real you. No matter how cool it may seem to be anyone else, knowing the real, you are far cooler than any mountain you can climb. I promise.

Once you figure out the thing that makes your heartbeat, marry it. Hold tightly to it. Make it a passionate pursuit. Don't let anyone or anything get in the way of pursuing it. For several years, I had an amazing group of friends. We all took vacations together, had a group Facebook page, and spent most of our free time together. It was the tv sitcom friendship I always dreamt of. And then, things started to change, and that tight bond dissipated almost overnight. I can't explain why. But I know this: not everyone is meant to go where you are going. It does not make them bad people, or you are a bad person for leaving them behind. People come into our lives for a reason, a season, and a lifetime. If you stamp "lifetime" on every person you meet, you will never get to your next level. It is much the same way with jobs, hobbies, and neighborhoods. You must allow the seasons to change so that the fruit you are meant to bear can blossom.

I don't know what your journey has included up to now. I don't know what the next leg of your journey holds. I am not suggesting you turn your life upside down to find yourself like a remote control buried in the couch cushions. Maybe you need to run a marathon. Or run to Target and get new sheets. Maybe you should cut your hair. Or cut people out of your life who do not believe in you. I know that as much as you have been through, it is just the beginning. There is so much left for you to do. You have an entire lifetime left, however long you are granted on this earth, to grow, change, and make mistakes. And along the way, you will have moments of contentment basking in the sun, knowing you are exactly where you are supposed to be in that moment. And you will have moments where you may not recognize this new place in which you find yourself. Both are okay. And neither is ever permanent.

Even if your circumstances don't change, you can choose how to grow in them. On those days when you feel as if you can't go on, you can choose to wake up because tomorrow might be the day you change the world if you decide not to let the world change you today. Rise up! You don't even need to pack. Just put one foot in front of the other and commit to the taking a step. Taking one step today guarantees you wake up in a different place tomorrow. No matter where it leads, you will find pieces of yourself and make peace with yourself along the way.

"In the midst of winter, I found there was, within me, an invincible summer"
~ Albert Camus

Learn more about Dr. Kasi Howard here
www.kasihoward.com/about.html

or

Connect with her on Facebook
www.facebook.com/drkasihoward

or

Innova Recovery Center offers therapeutic support through telehealth and in-office visits. We would be honored to join you on your journey to healing.
Learn more at:
www.innovarecoverycenter.com

Made in the USA
Columbia, SC
05 November 2019